The Little French Lawyer

John Fletcher and Philip Massinger

THE

Little French Lawyer.

A

COMEDY.

Persons Represented in the Play.

Dinant, *a Gentleman that formerly loved, and still pretended to love* Lamira.

Cleremont, *a merry Gentleman, his Friend.*

Champernell, *a lame old Gentleman, Husband to* Lamira.

Vertaign, *a Noble-man, and a Judge.*

Beaupre, *Son to* Vertaign.

Verdone, *Nephew to* Champernell.

Monsieur La Writt, *a wrangling Advocate, or the Little Lawyer.*

Sampson, *a foolish Advocate, Kinsman to* Vertaign.

Provost.

Gentlemen.

Clients.

Servants.

WOMEN.

Lamira, *Wife to* Champernell, *and Daughter to* Vertaign.

Anabell, *Niece to* Champernell.

Old Lady, *Nurse to* Lamira.

Charlotte, *Waiting Gentlewoman to* Lamira.

The Scene France.

The principal Actors were,

Joseph Taylor.

John Lowin.

John Underwood.

Robert Benfield.

Nicholas Toolie.

William Egleston.

Richard Sharpe.

Thomas Holcomb.

CONTENTS

Prologue.

Actus Primus. Scena Prima.

Actus Secundus. Scena Prima.

Actus Tertius. Scena Prima.

Actus Quartus. Scena Prima.

Actus Quintus. Scena Prima.

Epilogue.

APPENDIX

Prologue.

To promise much, before a play begin,
And when 'tis done, ask pardon, were a sin
We'l not be guilty of: and to excuse
Before we know a fault, were to abuse
The writers and our selves, for I dare say
We all are fool'd if this be not a Play,
And such a play as shall (so should plays do)
Imp times dull wings, and make you merry too.
'Twas to that purpose writ, so we intend it
And we have our wisht ends, if you commend it.

Actus Primus. Scena Prima.

Enter Dinant, *a[n]d* Cleremont.

Din. Disswade me not.

Clere. It will breed a brawl.

Din. I care not, I wear a Sword.

Cler. And wear discretion with it,
Or cast it off, let that direct your arm,
'Tis madness else, not valour, and more base
Than to receive a wrong.

Din. Why would you have me
Sit down with a disgrace, and thank the doer?
We are not Stoicks, and that passive courage
Is only now commendable in Lackies,
Peasants, and Tradesmen, not in men of rank
And qualitie, as I am.

Cler. Do not cherish
That daring vice, for which the whole age suffers.
The blood of our bold youth, that heretofore
Was spent in honourable action,
Or to defend, or to enlarge the Kingdom,
For the honour of our Country, and our Prince,
Pours it self out with prodigal expence
Upon our Mothers lap, the Earth that bred us
For every trifle; and these private Duells,
Which had their first original from the *Fr[enc]h*
(And for which, to this day, we are justly censured)
Are banisht from all civil Governments:
Scarce three in *Venice*, in as many years;
In *Florence*, they are rarer, and in all
The fair Dominions of the *Spanish* King,
They are never heard of: Nay, those neighbour Countries,
Which gladly imitate our other follies,
And come at a dear rate to buy them of us,
Begin now to detest them.

2

Din. Will you end yet—

Cler. And I have heard that some of our late Kings,
For the lie, wearing of a Mistris favour,
A cheat at Cards or Dice, and such like causes,
Have lost as many gallant Gentlemen,
As might have met the great *Turk* in the field
With confidence of a glorious Victorie,
And shall we then—

Din. No more, for shame no more,
Are you become a Patron too? 'tis a new one,
No more on't, burn't, give it to some Orator,
To help him to enlarge his exercise,
With such a one it might do well, and profit
The Curat of the Parish, but for *Cleremont*,
The bold, and undertaking *Cleremont*,
To talk thus to his friend, his friend that knows him,
Dinant that knows his *Cleremont*, is absurd,
And meer Apocrypha.

Cler. Why, what know you of me?

Din. Why if thou hast forgot thy self, I'le tell thee,
And not look back, to speak of what thou wert
At fifteen, for at those years I have heard
Thou wast flesh'd, and enter'd bravely.

Cler. Well Sir, well.

Din. But yesterday, thou wast the common second,
Of all that only knew thee, thou hadst bills
Set up on every post, to give thee notice
Where any difference was, and who were parties;
And as to save the charges of the Law
Poor men seek arbitrators, thou wert chosen
By such as knew thee not, to compound quarrels:
But thou wert so delighted with the sport,
That if there were no just cause, thou wouldst make one,
Or be engag'd thy self: This goodly calling
Thou hast followed five and twenty years, and studied
The Criticismes of contentions, and art thou
In so few hours transform'd? certain this night

3

Thou hast had strange dreams, or rather visions.

Clere. Yes, Sir,
I have seen fools, and fighters, chain'd together,
And the Fighters had the upper hand, and whipt first,
The poor Sots laughing at 'em. What I have been
It skils not, what I will be is resolv'd on.

Din. Why then you'l fight no more?

Cler. Such is my purpose.

Din. On no occasion?

Cler. There you stagger me.
Some kind of wrongs there are which flesh and blood
Cannot endure.

Din. Thou wouldst not willingly
Live a protested coward, or be call'd one?

Cler. Words are but words.

Din. Nor wouldst thou take a blow?

Cler. Not from my friend, though drunk, and from an enemy
I think much less.

Din. There's some hope of thee left then,
Wouldst thou hear me behind my back disgrac'd?

Cler. Do you think I am a rogue? they that should do it
Had better been born dumb.

Din. Or in thy presence
See me o'recharg'd with odds?

Cler. I'd fall my self first.

Din. Would'st thou endure thy Mistris be taken from thee,
And thou sit quiet?

Cler. There you touch my honour,

4

No French-man can endure that.

Di[n]. Pl—— upon thee,
Why dost thou talk of Peace then? that dar'st suffer
Nothing, or in thy self, or in thy friend
That is unmanly?

Cler. That I grant, I cannot:
But I'le not quarrel with this Gentleman
For wearing stammel Breeches, or this Gamester
For playing a thousand pounds, that owes me nothing;
For this mans taking up a common Wench
In raggs, and lowsie, then maintaining her
Caroach'd in cloth of Tissue, nor five hundred
Of such like toyes, that at no part concern me;
Marry, where my honour, or my friend is questioned,
I have a Sword, and I think I may use it
To the cutting of a Rascals throat, or so,
Like a good Christian.

Din. Thou art of a fine Religion,
And rather than we'l make a Schism in friendship
I will be of it: But to be serious,
Thou art acquainted with my tedious love-suit
To fair *Lamira*?

Cler. Too well Sir, and remember
Your presents, courtship, that's too good a name,
Your slave-like services, your morning musique;
Your walking three hours in the rain at midnight,
To see her at her window, sometimes laugh'd at,
Sometimes admitted, and vouchsaf'd to kiss
Her glove, her skirt, nay, I have heard, her slippers,
How then you triumph'd?
Here was love forsooth.

Din. These follies I deny not,
Such a contemptible thing my dotage made me,
But my reward for this—

Cler. As you deserv'd,
For he that makes a goddess of a Puppet,
Merits no other recompence.

Din. This day friend,
For thou art so—

Cler. I am no flatterer.

Din. This proud, ingratefull she, is married to
Lame *Champernel.*

Cler. I know him, he has been
As tall a Sea-man, and has thriv'd as well by't,
The loss of a legg and an arm deducted, as any
That ever put from *Marseilles*: you are tame,
Pl—— on't, it mads me; if it were my case,
I should kill all the family.

Din. Yet but now
You did preach patience.

Cler. I then came from confession,
And 'twas enjoyn'd me three hours for a penance,
To be a peaceable man, and to talk like one,
But now, all else being pardon'd, I begin
On a new Tally, Foot do any thing,
I'le second you.

Din. I would not willingly
Make red, my yet white conscience, yet I purpose
In the open street, as they come from the Temple,
(For this way they must pass,) to speak my wrongs,
And do it boldly.   [*Musick playes.*

Cler. Were thy tongue a Cannon,
I would stand by thee, boy, they come, upon 'em.

Din. Observe a little first.

Cler. This is fine fidling.

   Enter Vertaign, Champernel, Lamira, *Nurse*, Beaupre,   Verdone. *An
Epithalamium.*

6

SONG at the Wedding.

Come away, bring on the Bride
And place her by her Lovers side:
You fair troop of Maids attend her,
Pure and holy thoughts befriend her.
Blush, and wish, you Virgins all,
Many such fair nights may fall.

Chorus.

Hymen, fill the house with joy,
All thy sacred fires employ:
Bless the Bed with holy love,
Now fair orb of Beauty move.

Din. Stand by, for I'le be heard.

Verta. This is strange rudeness.

Din. 'Tis courtship, ballanced with injuries,
You all look pale with guilt, but I will dy
Your cheeks with blushes, if in your sear'd veins
There yet remain so much of honest blood
To make the colour; first to ye my Lord,
The Father of this Bride, whom you have sent
Alive into her grave.

Champ. How? to her grave?

Dina. Be patient Sir, I'le speak of you anon
You that allow'd me liberal access,
To make my way with service, and approv'd of
My birth, my person, years, and no base fortune:
You that are rich, and but in this held wise too,
That as a Father should have look'd upon
Your Daughter in a husband, and aim'd more
At what her youth, and heat of blood requir'd
In lawfull pleasures, than the parting from
Your Crowns to pay her dowr: you that already
Have one foot in the grave, yet study profit,
As if you were assur'd to live here ever;
What poor end had you, in this choice? in what

Deserve I your contempt? my house, and honours
At all parts equal yours, my fame as fair,
And not to praise my self, the City ranks me
In the first file of her most hopefull Gentry:
But *Champernel* is rich, and needs a nurse,
And not your gold: and add to that, he's old too,
His whole estate in likelihood to descend
Upon your Family; Here was providence,
I grant, but in a Nobleman base thrift:
No Merchants, nay, no Pirats, sell for Bondmen
Their Country-men, but you, a Gentleman,
To save a little gold, have sold your Daughter
To worse than slaverie.

Cler. This was spoke home indeed.

Beau. Sir, I shall take some other time to tell you,
That this harsh language was delivered to
An old man, but my Father.

Din. At your pleasure.

Cler. Proceed in your design, let me alone,
To answer him, or any man.

Verd. You presume
Too much upon your name, but may be couzen'd.

Din. But for you, most unmindfull of my service,
For now I may upbraid you, and with honour,
Since all is lost, and yet I am a gainer,
In being deliver'd from a torment in you,
For such you must have been, you to whom nature
Gave with a liberal hand most excellent form,
Your education, language, and discourse,
And judgement to distinguish, when you shall
With feeling sorrow understand how wretched
And miserable you have made your self,
And but your self have nothing to accuse,
Can you with hope from any beg compassion?
But you will say, you serv'd your Fathers pleasure,
Forgetting that unjust commands of Parents
Are not to be obey'd, or that you are rich,

8

And that to wealth all pleasure else are servants,
Yet but consider, how this wealth was purchas'd,
'Twill trouble the possession.

Champ. You Sir know
I got it, and with honour.

Din. But from whom?
Remember that, and how: you'l come indeed
To houses bravely furnish'd, but demanding
Where it was bought, this Souldier will not lie,
But answer truly, this rich cloth of Arras
I made my prize in such a Ship, this Plate
Was my share in another; these fair Jewels,
Coming a shore, I got in such a Village,
The Maid, or Matron kill'd, from whom they were ravish'd,
The Wines you drink are guilty too, for this,
This *Candie* Wine, three Merchants were undone,
These Suckets break as many more: in brief,
All you shall wear, or touch, or see, is purchas'd
By lawless force, and you but revel in
The tears, and grones of such as were the owners.

Champ. 'Tis false, most basely false.

Verta. Let losers talk.

Din. Lastly, those joyes, those best of joyes, which *Hymen*
Freely bestows on such, that come to tye
The sacred knot be blesses, won unto it
By equal love, and mutual affection,
Not blindly led with the desire of riches,
Most miserable you shall never taste of.
This Marriage night you'l meet a Widows bed,
Or failing of those pleasures all Brides look for,
Sin in your wish it were so.

Champ. Thou art a Villain,
A base, malitious slanderer.

Cler. Strike him.

Din. No, he is not worth a blow.

Champ. O that I had thee
In some close vault, that only would yield room
To me to use my Sword, to thee no hope
To run away, I would make thee on thy knees,
Bite out the tongue that wrong'd me.

Verta. Pray you have patience.

Lamira. This day I am to be your Soveraign,
Let me command you.

Champ. I am lost with rage,
And know not what I am my self, nor you:
Away, dare such as you, that love the smoke
Of peace more than the fire of glorious War,
And like unprofitable drones, feed on
Your grandsires labours, that, as I am now,
Were gathering Bees, and fill'd their Hive, this Country
With brave triumphant spoils, censure our actions?
You object my prizes to me, had you seen
The horrour of a Sea-fight, with what danger
I made them mine; the fire I fearless fought in,
And quench'd it in mine enemies blood, which straight
Like oyle pour'd out on't, made it burn anew;
My Deck blown up, with noise enough to mock
The lowdest thunder, and the desperate fools
That Boorded me, sent, to defie the tempests
That were against me, to the angrie Sea,
Frighted with men thrown o're; no victory,
But in despight of the four Elements,
The Fire, the Air, the Sea, and sands hid in it
To be atchiev'd, you would confess poor men,
(Though hopeless, such an honourable way
To get or wealth, or honour) in your selves
He that through all these dreadfull passages
Pursued and overtook them, unaffrighted,
Deserves reward, and not to have it stil'd
By the base name of theft.

Din. This is the Courtship,
That you must look for, Madam.

Cler. 'Twill do well,

When nothing can be done, to spend the night with:
Your tongue is sound good Lord, and I could wish
For this young Ladyes sake this leg, this arm,
And there is something else, I will not name,
(Though 'tis the only thing that must content her)
Had the same vigour.

Champ. You shall buy these scoffs
With your best blood: help me once noble anger,
(Nay stir not, I alone must right my self)
And with one leg transport me, to correct
These scandalous praters: O that noble wounds   [*Falls.*
Should hinder just revenge! D'ye jear me too?
I got these, not as you do, your diseases
In Brothels, or with riotous abuse
Of wine in Taverns; I have one leg shot,
One arm disabled, and am honour'd more,
By losing them, as I did, in the face
Of a brave enemy, than if they were
As when I put to Sea; you are *French-men* only,
In that you have been laied, and cur'd, goe to:
You mock my leg, but every bone about you,
Makes you good Almanack-makers, to foretell
What weather we shall have.

Din. Put up your Sword.

Cler. Or turn it to a Crutch, there't may b[e] usefull,
And live on the relation to your Wife
Of what a brave man you were once.

Din. And tell her,
What a fine vertue 'tis in a young Lady
To give an old man pap.

Cler. Or hire a Surgeon
To teach her to roul up your broken limbs.

Din. To make a Pultess, and endure the scent
Of oils, and nasty Plasters.

Verta. Fie Sir, fie,
You that have stood all dangers of all kinds, to

Yield to a Rivalls scoffe?

Lamira. Shed tears upon
Your Wedding day? this is unmanly Gentlemen.

Champ. They are tears of anger: O that I should live
To play the woman thus! All powerfull heaven,
Restore me, but one hour, that strength again,
That I had once, to chastise in these men
Their folies, and ill manners, and that done,
When you please, I'le yield up the fort of life,
And do it gladly.

Cler. We ha' the better of him,
We ha' made him cry.

Verdo. You shall have satisfaction.
And I will do it nobly, or disclaim me.

Beaup. I say no more, you have a Brother, Sister,
This is your wedding day, we are in the street,
And howsoever they forget their honour,
'Tis fit I lose not mine, by their example.

Vert. If there be Laws in *Paris,* look to answer
This insolent affront.

Cler. You that live by them,
Study 'em for heavens sake; for my part I know not
Nor care not what they are. Is the[re] ought else
That you would say;

Din. Nothing, I have my ends.
Lamira weeps, I have said too much I fear;
So dearly once I lov'd her, that I cannot
Endure to see her tears.   [*Exeunt* Dinant, *and* Cleremont.

Champ. See you perform it,
And do it like my Nephew.

Verdo. If I fail in't
Ne'r know me more, Cousin *Beaupre.*

12

Champ. Repent not
What thou hast done, my life, thou shalt not find
I am decrepit; in my love and service,
I will be young, and constant, and believe me,
For thou shalt find it true, in scorn of all
The scandals these rude men have thrown upon me
I'le meet thy pleasures with a young mans ardour,
And in all circumstances of a Husband,
Perform my part.

Lamira. Good Sir, I am your servant,
And 'tis too late now, if I did repent,
(Which as I am a virgin yet, I do not)
To undoe the knot, that by the Church is tyed.
Only I would beseech ye, as you have
A good opinion of me, and my vertues,
For so you have pleas'd to stile my innocent weakness,
That what hath pass'd be[t]ween *Dinant* and me,
Or what now in your hearing he hath spoken,
Beget not doubts, or fears.

Champ. I apprehend you,
You think I will be jealous; as I live
Thou art mistaken sweet; and to confirm it
Discourse with whom thou wilt, ride where thou wilt,
Feast whom thou wilt, as often as thou wilt,
For I will have no other guards upon thee
Than thine own thoughts.

Lamira. I'le use this liberty
With moderation Sir.

Beaup. I am resolv'd.
Steal off, I'le follow you.

Champ. Come Sir, you droop;
Till you find cause, which I shall never give,
Dislike not of your Son in Law.

Verta. Sir, you teach me
The language I should use; I am most happy
In being so near you.   [*Exeunt* Verdone, *and* Beaupre.

Lamira. O my fears! good nurse
Follow my Brother unobserv'd, and learn
Which way he takes.

Nurs. I will be carefull Madam.　　　[*Exit* Nurse.

Champ. Between us complements are superfluous,
On Gentlemen, th' affront we have met here
We'l think upon hereafter, 'twere unfit
To cherish any thought to breed unrest,
Or to our selves, or to our Nuptial feast.　　　[*Exeunt.*

　　Enter Dinant, *and* Cleremont.

Cler. We shall have sport, ne'r fear't.

Din. What sport I prethee?

Cler. Why we must fight, I know it, and I long for't,
It was apparent in the fiery eye
Of young *Verdone*, *Beaupre* look'd pale and shook too,
Familiar signs of anger. They are both brave fellows
Tri'd and approv'd, and I am proud to encounter
With men, from whom no honour can be lost;
They will play up to a man, and set him off.
When e're I go to the field, heaven keep me from
The meeting of an unflesh'd youth or, Coward,
The first, to get a name, comes on too hot,
The Coward is so swift in giving ground,
There is no overtaking him without
A hunting Nag, well breath'd too.

Din. All this while,
You ne'r think on the danger.

Cler. Why 'tis no more
Than meeting of a dozen friends at Supper,
And drinking hard; mischief comes there unlook'd for,
I am sure as suddain, and strikes home as often,
For this we are prepar'd.

Din. Lamira Loves
Her Brother *Beaupre* dearly.

14

Cler. What of that?

Din. And should he call me to account for what
But now I spake, nor can I with mine honour
Recant my words, that little hope is left me,
E're to enjoy what (next to Heaven) I long for,
Is taken from me.

Cer. Why what can you hope for,
She being now married?

Din. Oh my *Cleremont*,
To you all secrets of my heart lye open,
And I rest most secure that whatsoe're
I lock up there, is as a private thought,
And will no farther wrong me. I am a *French-man*,
And for the greater part we are born Courtiers,
She is a woman, and however yet,
No heat of service had the power to melt
Her frozen Chastity, time and opportunitie
May work her to my ends, I confess ill ones,
And yet I must pursue 'em: now her marriage,
In probabilitie, will no way hurt,
But rather help me.

Cler. Sits the wind there? pray you tell me
How far off dwells your love from lust?

Din. Too near,
But prethee chide me not.

Cler. Not I, goe on boy,
I have faults my self, and will not reprehend
A crime I am not free from: for her Marriage,
I do esteem it (and most batchellors are
Of my opinion) as a fair protection,
To play the wanton without loss of honour.

Din. Would she make use of't so, I were most happy.

Cler. No more of this. Judge now,
Whether I have the gift of prophecie.

Enter Beaupre, *and* Verdone.

Beaup. Monsieur *Dinant*,
I am glad to find you, Sir.

Din. I am at your service.

Verd. Good Monsieur *Cleremont*, I have long wish'd
To be known better to you.

Cler. My desires
Embrace your wishes Sir.

Beaup. Sir, I have ever
Esteem'd you truly noble, and profess
I should have been most proud, to have had the honour
To call you Brother, but my Fathers pleasure
Denied that happiness. I know no man lives,
That can command his passions, and therefore
Dare not condemn the late intemperate language
You were pleas'd to use to my Father and my Sister,
He's old and she a woman, I most sorrie
My honour does compel me to entreat you,
To do me the favour, with your sword to meet me
A mile without the Citie.

Din. You much honour me.
In the demand, I'le gladly wait upon you.

Beaup. O Sir you teach me what to say: the time?

Din. With the next Sun, if you think fit.

Beaup. The place?

Din. Near to the vineyard eastward from the Citie.

Beaup. I like it well, this Gentleman if you please
Will keep me company.

Cler. That is agreed on;
And in my friends behalf I will attend him.

Verd. You shall not miss my service.

Beaup. Good day Gentlemen.   [*Ex.* Beaup. *and* Verd.

Din. At your Commandment.

Cler. Proud to be your servants.
I think there is no Nation under Heaven
That cut their enemies throats with complement,
And such fine tricks as we do: If you have
Any few Prayers to say, this night you may
Call 'em to mind and use 'em, for my self,
As I have little to lose, my care is less,
So till to morrow morning I bequeath you
To your devotions; and those paid, but use
That noble courage I have seen, and we
Shall fight, as in a Castle.

Din. Thou art all honour,
Thy resolution would steel a Coward,
And I most fortunate in such a Friend;
All tenderness and nice respect of woman
Be now far from me, reputation take
A full possession of my heart, and prove
Honour the first place holds, the second Love.   [*Exeunt.*

     Enter Lamira, Charlote.

Lami. Sleeps my Lord still, *Charlote*?

Char. Not to be wak'd.
By your Ladiships cheerfull looks I well perceive
That this night the good Lord hath been
At an unusual service, and no wonder
If he rest after it.

Lamira. You are very bold.

Char. Your Creature Madam, and when you are pleas'd
Sadness to me's a stranger, your good pardon
If I speak like a fool, I could have wisht
To have ta'ne your place to night, had bold *Dinant*
Your first and most obsequious servant tasted

Those delicates, which by his lethargie
As it appears, have cloy'd my Lord.

Lamira. No, more.

Char. I am silenc'd, Madam.

Lamira. Saw you my nurse this morning?

Charl. No Madam.

Lamira. I am full of fears.   [*Knock within.*
Who's that?

Charl. She you enquir'd for.

Lamira. Bring her in, and leave me.   [*Exit* Charlote.
Now nurse what news?

    Enter Nurse.

Nurse. O Ladie dreadfull ones.
They are to fight this morning, there's no remedie.
I saw my Lord your Brother, and *Verdone*
Take horse as I came by.

Lamira. Where's *Cleremont*?

Nurse. I met him too, and mounted.

Lamira. Where's *Dinant*?

Nurse. There's all the hope, I have staid him with a trick,
If I have done well so.

Lamira. What trick?

Nurse. I told him,
Your Ladiship laid your command upon him,
To attend you presently, and to confirm it,
Gave him the ring he oft hath seen you wear,
That you bestowed on me: he waits without
Disguis'd, and if you have that power in him,

18

As I presume you have, it is in you
To stay or alter him.

Lamira. Have you learnt the place,
Where they are to encounter?

Nurse. Yes 'tis where
The Duke of *Burgundie* met *Lewis* th' eleventh.

Lamir. Enough, I will reward thee liberally,   [*Exit* Nurse.
Goe bring him in: full dear I loved *Dinant,*
While it was lawfull, but those fires are quench'd
I being now anothers, truth forgive me
And let dissimulation be no crime,
Though most unwillingly I put it on
To guard a Brothers safetie.

   Enter Dinant.

Din. Now your pleasure,
Though ill you have deserv'd it, you perceive
I am still your fool, and cannot but obey
What ever you command.

Lamira. You speak, as if
You did repent it, and 'tis not worth my thanks then,
But there has been a time, in which you would
Receive this as a favour.

Din. Hope was left then
Of recompence.

Lamira. Why I am still *Lamira,*
And you *Dinant,* and 'tis yet in my power,
I dare not say I'le put it into act,
To reward your love and service.

Din. There's some comfort.

Lami. But think not that so low I prize my fame,
To give it up to any man that refuses
To buy it, or with danger of performance
Of what I shall enjoin him.

Din. Name that danger
Be it of what horrid shape soever Ladie
Which I will shrink at; only at this instant
Be speedie in't.

Lamira. I'le put you to the trial:
You shall not fight to day, do you start at that?
Not with my Brother, I have heard your difference,
Mine is no *Helens* beauty to be purchas'd
With blood, and so defended, if you look for
Favours from me, deserve them with obedience,
There's no way else to gain 'em.

Din. You command
What with mine honour I cannot obey,
Which lies at pawn against it, and a friend
Equally dear as that, or life, engag'd,
Not for himself, but me.

Lamira. Why, foolish man,
Dare you solicite me to serve your lust,
In which not only I abuse my Lord,
My Father, and my family, but write whore,
Though not upon my forehead, in my conscience,
To be read hourly, and yet name your honour?
Yours suffers but in circumstance; mine in substance.
If you obey me, you part with some credit,
From whom? the giddy multitude; but mankind
Will censure me, and justly.

Din. I will lose,
What most I do desire, rather than hazard
So dear a friend, or write my self a coward,
'Tis better be no man.

Lamira. This will not do;
Why, I desire not, you should be a coward,
Nor do I weigh my Brothers life with yours,
Meet him, fight with him, do, and kill him fairly,
Let me not suffer for you, I am careless.

Din. Suffer for me?

Lamira. For you, my kindness to you
Already brands me with a strumpets name.

Din. O that I knew the wretch!

Lamira. I will not name him,
Nor give you any Character to know him;
But if you dare, and instantly ride forth
At the west port of the City, and defend there
My reputation, against all you meet,
For two hours only, I'le not swear *Dinant*,
To satisfie, (though sure I think I shall)
What ever you desire, if you denie this,
Be desperate, for willingly, by this light,
I'le never see thee more.

Din. Two hours, do you say?

Lamira. Only two hours.

Din. I were no Gentleman,
Should I make scruple of it; this favour arms me,
And boldly I'll perform it.   [*Exit.*

Lamira. I am glad on't.
This will prevent their meeting yet, and keep
My Brother safe, which was the mark I shot at.   [*Exit.*

Actus Secundus. Scena Prima.

Enter Cleremont, *as in the field.*

Cler. I am first i'th' field, that honour's gain'd of our side,
Pray Heaven I may get off as honourablie,
The hour is past, I wonder *Dinant* comes not,
This is the place, I cannot see him yet;
It is his quarel too that brought me hither,
And I ne'r knew him yet, but to his honour
A firm and worthy Friend, yet I see nothing,
Nor Horse nor man, 'twould vex me to be left here,
To th' mercy of two swords, and two approv'd ones.
I never knew him last.

Enter Beaupre, *and* Verdone.

Beaup. You are well met *Cleremont.*

Verdo. You are a fair Gentleman, and love your friend Sir.
What are you ready? the time has overta'ne us.

Beaup. And this you know the place.

Cler. No *Dinant* yet?

Beaup. We come not now to argue, but to do;
We wait you Sir.

Cler. There's no time past yet Gentlemen,
We have day enough: is't possible he comes not?
You see I am ready here, and do but stay
Till my Friend come, walk but a turn or two,
'Twill not be long.

Verd. We came to fight.

Cler. Ye shall fight Gentlemen,
And fight enough, but a short turn or two,
I think I see him, set up your watch, we'l fight by it.

Beaup. That is not he; we will not be deluded.

22

Cler. Am I bob'd thus? pray take a pipe of tobacco,
Or sing but some new air; by that time, Gentlemen—

Verd. Come draw your Sword, you know the custome here Sir,
First come, first serv'd.

Cler. Though it be held a custom,
And practised so, I do not hold it honest;
What honour can you both win on me single?

Beaup. Yield up your Sword then.

Cler. Yield my Sword? that's Hebrew;
I'le be first cut a p[iec]es; hold but a while,
I'le take the next that comes.

   Enter an old Gentleman.

You are an old Gentleman?

Gent. Yes indeed am I, Sir.

Cler. And wear no Sword?

Gent. I need none, Sir.

Cler. I would you did, and had one;
I want now such a foolish courtesie.
You see these Gentlemen?

Gent. You want a second.
In good Faith Sir, I was never handsom at it,
I would you had my Son, but he's in *Italy*,
A proper Gentleman; you may do well gallants
If your quarrel be not capital, to have more mercy,
The Gentleman may do his Country—

Cler. Now I beseech you, Sir,
If you dare not fight, do not stay to beg my pardon.
There lies your way.

Gent. Good morrow Gentlemen.   [*Exit.*

Verd. You see your fortune,
You had better yield your Sword.

Cler. Pray ye stay a little.

   Enter two Gentlemen.

Upon mine honestie, you shall be fought with;
Well, *Dinant*, well, these wear swords and seem brave fellows.
As you are Gentlemen, one of you supply me.
I want a Second now to meet these gallants,
You know what honour is.

1 Gent. Sir you must pardon us,
We goe about the same work, you are ready for;
And must fight presently, else we were your servants.

2 Gent. God speed you, and good day.   [*Exit* Gent.

Cler. Am I thus Colted?

Beaup. Come either yield—

Cler. As you are honest Gentlemen,
Stay but the next, and then I'le take my fortune,
And if I fight not like a man—Fy *Dinant*,
Cold now and treacherous.

   Enter Monsieur La-writ, *within.*

La-Writ. I understand your causes.
Yours about corn, yours about pins and glasses,
Will you make me mad, have I not all the parcells?
And his Petition too, about Bell-founding?
Send in your witnesses, what will you have me do?
Will you have me break my heart? my brains are melted;
And tell your Master, as I am a Gentleman,
His Cause shall be the first, commend me to your Mistris,
And tell her, if there be an extraordinary feather,
And tall enough for her—I shall dispatch you too,
I know your cause, for transporting of Farthingales
Trouble me no more, I say again to you,
No more vexation: bid my wife send me some puddings;

24

I have a Cause to run through, requires puddings,
Puddings enough. Farewel.

Cler. God speed you, Sir.

Beaup. Would he would take this fellow.

Verd. A rare Youth.

Cler. If you be not hastie, Sir.

La-writ. Yes, I am hastie,
Exceeding hastie, Sir, I am going to the Parliament,
You understand this bag, if you have any business
Depending there, be short, and let me hear it,
And pay your Fees.

Cler. 'Faith, Sir, I have a business,
But it depends upon no Parliament.

La-writ. I have no skill in't then.

Cler. I must desire you,
'Tis a Sword matter, Sir.

La-writ. I am no Cutler,
I am an Advocate, Sir.

Beaup. How the thing looks?

Verd. When he brings him to fight.

Cler. Be not so hastie,
You wear a good Sword.

La-writ. I know not that,
I never drew it yet, or whether it be a Sword—

Cler. I must entreat you try, Sir, and bear a part
Against these Gentlemen, I want a second;
Ye seem a man, and 'tis a noble office.

La-writ. I am a Lawyer, Sir, I am no fighter.

Cler. You that breed quarels, Sir, know best to satisfie.

Beaup. This is some sport yet.

Verd. If this fellow should fight.

La-writ. And for any thing I know, I am an arrant coward,
Do not trust me, I think I am a coward.

Cler. Try, try, you are mistaken: walk on Gentlemen,
The man shall follow presently.

La-writ. Are ye mad Gentleman?
My business is within this half hour.

Cler. That's all one,
We'll dispatch within this quarter, there in that bottom,
'Tis most convenient Gentlemen.

Beaup. Well, we'll wait, Sir.

Verd. Why this will be a comick fight, you'l follow.

La-writ. As I am a true man, I cannot fight.
                    [*Ex.* Beaupre, Verdone.

Cler. Away, away,
I know you can: I like your modesty,
I know you will fight and so fight, with such metal,
And with such judgement meet your enemies fury;
I see it in your eye, Sir.

La-writ. I'le be hang'd then;
And I charge you in the Kings name, name no more fighting.

Cler. I charge you in the Kings name, play the man,
Which if you do not quickly, I begin with you,
I'le make you dance, do you see your fiddlestick?
Sweet A[d]vocate thou shalt fight.

La-writ. Stand farther Gentleman,
Or I'le give you such a dust o'th' chapps—

Cler. Spoke bravely,
And like thy self, a noble Advocate:
Come to thy tools.

La-writ. I do not say I'le fight;

Cler. I say thou shalt, and bravely.

La-writ. If I do fight;
I say, if I do, but do not depend upon't,
And yet I have a foolish itch upon me,
What shall become of my Writings?

Cler. Let 'em ly by,
They will not run away, man.

La-writ. I may be kill'd too,
And where are all my causes then? my business?
I will not fight, I cannot fight, my Causes—

Cler. Thou shalt fight, if thou hadst a thousand causes,
Thou art a man to fight for any cause,
And carry it with honour.

La-writ. Hum, say you so? if I should
Be such a coxcombe to prove valiant now—

Cler. I know thou art most valiant.

La-writ. Do you think so?
I am undone for ever, if it prove so,
I tell you that, my honest friend, for ever;
For I shall ne're leave quarrelling.
How long must we fight? for I cannot stay,
Nor will not stay, I have business.

Cler. We'l do't in a minute, in a moment.

La-writ. Here will I hang my bag then, it may save my belly,
I never lov'd cold Iron there.

Cler. You do wisely.

La-writ. Help me to pluck my Sword out then, quickly, quickly,
'Thas not seen Sun these ten years.

Cler. How it grumbles!
This Sword is vengeance angry.

La-writ. Now I'le put my hat up,
And say my prayers as I goe; away boy,
If I be kill'd, remember the little Lawyer.   [*Exeunt.*

    Enter Beaupre.

Beaup. They are both come on, that may be a stubborn rascal,
Take you that ground,

    Enter La-writ.

I'le stay here, fight bravely.

La-writ. To't chearfully my boyes, you'l let's have fair play,
None of your foyning tricks.

Beaup. Come forward Monsieur;   [*Fight.*
What hast thou there? a pudding in thy belly?
I shall see what it holds.

La-writ. Put your spoon home then:
Nay, since I must fight, have at you without wit, Sir:
God a mercy bagg.

Beaup. Nothing but bumbast in ye?
The Rogue winks and fights.

La-writ. Now your fine fencing, Sir: [*Beau. loses his sword.*
Stand off, thou diest on point else,   [*La-writ treads on it.*
I have it, I have it: yet further off:
I have his Sword.

Cler. Then keep it, be sure you keep it.

La-writ. I'le put it in my mouth else.
Stand further off yet, and stand quietly,
And look another way, or I'le be with you,

Is this all? I'le undertake within these two daies
To furnish any Cutler in this Kingdom.

Beau. Pox, what fortune's this? disarm'd by a puppie?
A snail? a Dog?

La-writ. No more o' these words Gentleman,
Sweet Gentleman no more, do not provoke me,
Go walk i'th' horse-fair; whistle Gentleman,
What must I do now?

   Enter Cleremont, *pursued by* Verdone.

Cler. Help me, I am almost breathless.

La-writ. With all my heart, there's a cold pye for you, Sir.

Cler. Thou strik'st me, fool.

La-writ. Thou fool, stand further off then,
Deliver, deliver.

Cler. Hold fast.   [*He strikes up the others heels,*
                  and takes his Sword too.
La-writ. I never fail in't,
There's twelve pence, go buy you two leaden Daggers,
Have I done well?

Cler. Most like a Gentleman.

Beau. And we two basely lost.

Verd. 'Tis but a fortune,
We shall yet find an hour.   [*Ex.* Beau. Verd. *sad.*

Cler. I shall be glad on't.

La-writ. Where's my cloak, and my trinkets?
Or will you fight any longer, for a crash or two?

Cler. I am your noble friend, Sir.

La-writ. It may be so.

Cler. What honour shall I do you,
For this great courtesie?

La-writ. All I desire of ye,
Is to take the quarrel to your self, and let me hear no more on't,
I have no liking to't, 'tis a foolish matter,
And help me to put up my Sword.

Cler. Most willingly.
But I am bound to gratifie you, and I must not leave you.

La-writ. I tell you, I will not be gratified,
Nor I will hear no more on't: take the Swords too,
And do not anger me but leave me quietly.
For the matter of honour, 'tis at your own disposure,
And so, and so.   [*Exit* La-writ.

Cler. This is a most rare Lawyer:
I am sure most valiant. Well *Dinant*, as you satisfie me,
I say no more: I am loaden like an Armorer.   [*Exit* Cler.

   Enter Dinant.

Din. To be dispatcht upon a sleeveless errand?
To leave my friend engag'd, mine honour tainted?
These are trim things. I am set here like a Perdue,
To watch a fellow, that has wrong'd my Mistris,
A scurvy fellow that must pass this way,
But what this scurvy fellow is, or whence,
Or whether his name be *William* or *John*,
Or *Anthony* or *Dick*, or any thing, I know not;
A scurvy rascally fellow I must aim at,
And there's the office of an Asse flung on me.
Sure *Cleremont* has fought, but how come off,
And what the world shall think of me hereafter:
Well, woman, woman, I must look your rascals,
And lose my reputation: ye have a fine power over us.
These two long hours I have trotted here, and curiously
Survey'd all goers by, yet find no rascal,
Nor any face to quarel with:
What's that?   [La-writ *sings within, then Enters.*
This is a rascally voice, sure it comes this way.

La-writ. He strook so hard, the Bason broke,
        And Tarquin *heard the sound.*

Din. What Mister thing is this? let me survey it.

La-writ. And then he strook his neck in two.

Din. This may be a rascal, but 'tis a mad rascal,
What an Alphabet of faces he puts on!
Hey how it fences! if this should be the rogue,
As 'tis the likeliest rogue I see this day —

La-wr. Was ever man for Ladies sake? down, down.

Di. And what are you good Sir? down, down, down, down.

La-writ. What's that to you good Sir? down, down.

Din. A pox on you good Sir, down, down, down,
You with your Buckram bag, what make you here?
And from whence come you? I could fight with my shadow now.

La-wr. Thou fierce man that like Sir *Lancelot* dost appear,
I need not tell thee what I am, nor eke what I make here.

Din. This is a precious knave, stay, stay, good *Tristram,*
And let me ask thy mightiness a question,
Did ye never abuse a Lady?

La-writ. Not; to abuse a Lady, is very hard, Sir.

Din. Say you so, Sir?
Didst thou never abuse her honour?

La-writ. Not; to abuse her honour, is impossible.

Din. Certain this is the rascal: What's thy name?

La-writ. My name is *Cock o' two,* use me respectively,
I will be Cock of three else.

Din. What's all this?
You say, you did abuse a Lady.

La-writ. You ly.

Din. And that you wrong'd her honour.

La-writ. That's two lyes,
Speak suddenly, for I am full of business.

Din. What art thou, or what canst thou be, thou pea-goose,
That dar'st give me the ly thus? thou mak'st me wonder.

La-writ. And wonder on, till time make all things plain.

Din. You must not part so, Sir, art thou a Gentleman?

La-writ. Ask those upon whose ruins I am mounted.

Din. This is some Cavellero Knight o'th' Sun.

La-wr. I tell thee I am as good a Gentleman as the Duke;
I have atchieved — goe follow thy business.

Din. But for this Lady, Sir —

La-writ. Why, hang this Lady, Sir,
And the Lady Mother too, Sir, what have I to do with Ladies?

   Enter Cleremont.

Cler. 'Tis the little Lawyers voice: has he got my way?
It should be hereabouts.

Din. Ye dry bisket rogue,
I will so swinge you for this blasphemie —
Have I found you out?

Cler. That should be *Dinants* tongue too.

La-wr. And I defy thee do thy worst: *O ho quoth* Lancelot *tho.*
And that thou shalt know, I am a true Gentleman,
And speak according to the phrase triumphant;
Thy Lady is a scurvy Lady, and a shitten Lady,
And though I never heard of her, a deboshed Lady,
And thou, a squire of low degree; will that content thee?

32

Dost [thou] way-lay me with Ladies? A pretty sword, Sir,
A very pretty sword, I have a great mind to't.

Din. You shall not lose your longing, rogue.

Cler. Hold, hold.
Hold *Dinant*, as thou art a Gentleman.

La-writ. As much as you will, my hand is in now.

Cler. I am your friend, Sir: *Dinant* you draw your sword
Upon the Gentleman preserv'd your honour:
This was my second, and did back me nobly,
For shame forbear.

Din. I ask your mercy, Sir, and am your servant now.

La-writ. May we not fight then?

Cler. I am sure you shall not now.

La-wr. I am sorry for't, I am sure I'le stay no longer then,
Not a jot longer: are there any more on ye afore?
I will sing still, Sir.   [*Exit* La-writ, *singing.*

Din. I look now you should chide me, and 'tis fit,
And with much bitterness express your anger,
I have deserv'd: yet when you know—

Cler. I thank ye,
Do you think that the wrong you have off'red me,
The most unmanly wrong, unfriendly wrong—

Din. I do confess—

Cler. That boyish sleight—

Din. Not so, Sir.

Cler. That poor and base renouncing of your honour,
Can be allaied with words?

Din. I give you way still.

Cler. Coloured with smooth excuses? Was it a friends part,
A Gentlemans, a mans that wears a Sword,
And stands upon the point of reputation,
To hide his head then, when his honour call'd him?
Call'd him aloud, and led him to his fortune?
To halt and slip the coller? by my life,
I would have given my life I had never known thee,
Thou hast eaten Canker-like into my judgement
With this disgrace, thy whole life cannot heal again.

Din. This I can suffer too, I find it honest.

Cler. Can you pretend an excuse now may absolve you,
Or any thing like honest, to bring you off?
Ingage me like an Asse?

Din. Will you but hear me?

Cler. Expose me like a Jade to tug, and hale through,
Laugh'd at, and almost hooted? your disgraces
Invite mens Swords and angers to dispatch me.

Din. If you will be patient.

Cler. And be abus'd still: But that I have call'd thee friend,
And to that name allow a Sanctuary,
You should hear further from me, I would not talk thus:
But henceforth stand upon your own bottom, Sir,
And bear your own abuses, I scorn my sword
Should travel in so poor and empty quarrels.

Din. Ha' you done yet? take your whole swing of anger,
I'le bear all with content.

Cler. Why were you absent?

Din. You know I am no Coward, you have seen that,
And therefore, out of fear forsook you not:
You know I am not false, of a treacherous nature,
Apt to betray my friend, I have fought for you too;
You know no business, that concern'd my state,
My kindred, or my life.

Cler. Where was the fault then?

Din. The honour of that Lady I adore,
Her credit, and her name: ye know she sent for me,
And with what haste.

Cler. What was he that traduc'd?

Din. The man i'th' Moon, I think, hither I was sent,
But to what end—

   Enter old Lady.

Cler. This is a pretty flim-flam.

O. La. I am glad I have met you Sir, I have been seeking,
And seeking every where.

Cler. And now you have found him,
Declare what business, our Embassadour.

O. Lady. What's that to ye good man flouter? O Sir, my Lady.

Din. Prethee no more of thy Lady, I have too much on't.

Cler. Let me have a little, speak to me.

Old Lady. To you Sir?
'Tis more than time: All occasions set aside Sir,
Or whatsoever may be thought a business—

Din. What then?

Old Lady. Repair to me within this hour.

Cler. Where?

O. Lady. What's that to you? come you, Sir, when y'are sent for.

Cler. God a mercy *Mumpsimus*,
You may goe *Dinant*, and follow this old Fairie,
Till you have lost your self, your friends, your credit,
And Hunt away your youth in rare adventures,

The Little French Lawyer

I can but grieve I have known you.

Old Lady. Will ye goe Sir?
I come not often to you with these blessings,
You m[a]y believe that thing there, and repent it,
That dogged thing.

Cler. Peace touchwood.

Din. I will not goe:
Goe bid your Lady seek some fool to fawn on her,
Some unexperienc'd puppie to make sport with,
I have been her mirth too long, thus I shake from me
The fetters she put on; thus her enchantments
I blow away like wind, no more her beauty —

Old Lady. Take heed Sir what you say.

Cler. Goe forward, *Dinant.*

Din. The charms shot from her eyes —

Old Lady. Be wise.

Cler. Be Valiant.

Din. That tongue that tells fair tales to mens destructions
Shall never rack me more.

Old Lady. Stay there.

Cler. Goe forward.

Din. I will now hear her, see her as a woman,
Survey her, and the power man has allow'd, Sir,
As I would do the course of common things,
Unmov'd, unstruck.

Cler. Hold there, and I forgive thee.

Din. She is not fair, and that that makes her proud,
Is not her own, our eyes bestow it on her,
To touch and kiss her is no blessedness,

A Sun-burnt Ethiops lip's as soft as her's.
Goe bid her stick some other triumph up,
And take into her favour some dull fool,
That has no pretious time to lose, no friends,
No honour, nor no life, like a bold Merchant,
A bold and banquerupt man, I have ventur'd all these,
And split my bottom: return this answer to her,
I am awake again and see her mischiefs,
And am not now, on every idle errand,
And new coyn'd anger, to be hurried,
And then despis'd again, I have forgot her.

Cler. If this be true—

O. Lady. I am sorry, I have troubled you,
More sorrie, that my Lady has adventur'd
So great a favour in so weak a mind:
This hour you have refus'd that when you come to know it,
Will run you mad, and make you curse that fellow,
She is not fair, nor handsom, so I leave you.

Cler. Stay Lady, stay, but is there such a business?

O. Lady. You would break your neck 'twere yours.

Cler. My back, you would say.

O. La. But play the friends part still, Sir, and undoe him,
'Tis a fair office.

Din. I have spoke too liberally.

O. Lady. I shall deliver what you say.

Cler. You shall be hang'd first,
You would fain be prating now; take the man with you.

O. Lady. Not I, I have no power.

Cler. You may goe *Dinant.*

O. Lady. 'Tis in's own will, I had no further charge, Sir,
Than to tell him what I did, which if I had thought

It should have been receiv'd so—

Cler. 'Faith you may,
You do not know how far it may concern you.
If I perceiv'd any trick in't.

Din. 'Twill end there.

Cler. 'Tis my fault then, there is an hour in fortune,
That must be still observ'd: you think I'le chide you,
When things must be, nay see, an he will hold his head up?
Would such a Lady send, with such a charge too?
Say she has plaid the fool, play the fool with her again,
The great fool, the greater still the better.
He shall goe with you woman.

Old Lady. As it please him,
I know the way alone else.

Din. Where is your Lady?

O. Lady. I shall direct you quickly.

Din. Well, I'le goe,
But what her wrongs will give me leave to say.

Cler. We'll leave that to your selves: I shall hear from you.

Din. As soon as I come off—

Cler. Come on then bravely;
Farewel till then, and play the man.

Din. You are merry;
All I expect is scorn: I'le lead you Lady.   [*Exeunt severally.*

Actus Tertius. Scena Prima.

Enter Champernel, Lamira, Beaupre, Verdone, Charlotte.

Beaup. We'l venture on him.

Cham. Out of my doors I charge thee, see me no more.

Lami. Your Nephew?

Cham. I disclaim him,
He has no part in me, nor in my blood,
My Brother that kept fortune bound, and left
Conquest hereditary to his Issue
Could not beget a coward.

Verd. I fought, Sir,
Like a good fellow, and a Souldier too,
But men are men, and cannot make their fates:
Ascribe you to my Father what you please,
I am born to suffer.

Cham. All disgraces wretch.

Lam. Good Sir be patient.

Cham. Was there no tree,
(For to fall by a noble enemies sword,
A Coward is unworthy) nor no River,
To force thy life out backward or to drown it,
But that thou must survive thy i[n]famie?
And kill me with the sight of one I hate,
And gladly would forget?

Beaup. Sir, his misfortune
Deserves not this reproof.

Cham. In your opinion,
'Tis fit you two should be of one belief,
You are indeed fine gallants, and fight bravely
I'th' City with your tongues, but in the field
Have neither spirit to dare nor power to do,

The Little French Lawyer

Your swords are all lead there.

Beaup. I know no duty,
(How ever you may wreak your spleen on him,)
That bindes me to endure this.

Cham. From *Dinant*
You'l suffer more; that ever cursed I,
Should give my honour up, to the defence
Of such a thing as he is, or my Lady
That is all Innocent, for whom a dove would
Assume the courage of a daring Eagle,
Repose her confidence in one that can
No better guard her. In contempt of you
I love *Dinant*, mine enemy, nay admire him,
His valour claims it from me, and with justice,
He that could fight thus, in a cause not honest,
His sword edg'd with defence of right and honour,
Would pierce as deep as lightning, with that speed too,
And kill as deadly.

Verd. You are as far from justice
In him you praise, as equitie in the censure
You load me with.

Beaup. Dinant? he durst not meet us.

Lam. How? durst not, Brother?

Beaup. Durst not, I repeat it.

Verd. Nor was it *Cleremont*'s valour that disarm'd us,
I had the better of him; for *Dinant*,
If that might make my peace with you, I dare
Write him a Coward upon every post,
And with the hazard of my life defend it.

Lam. If 'twere laid at the stake you'd lose it, Nephew.

Cham. Came he not, say you?

Verd. No, but in his room,
There was a Devil, hir'd from some Magician

I'th' shape of an Atturney.

Beau. 'Twas he did it.

Verd. And his the honour.

Beau. I could wish *Dinant*—
But what talk I of one that stept aside,
And durst not come?

Lam. I am such a friend to truth,
I cannot hear this: why do you detract
Thus poorly (I should say to others basely)
From one of such approv'd worth?

Cham. Ha! how's this?

Lam. From one so excellent in all that's noble,
Whose only weakness is excess of courage?
That knows no enemies, that he cannot master,
But his affections, and in them, the worst
His love to me.

Cham. To you?

Lam. Yes, Sir, to me,
I dare (for what is that which Innocence dares not)
To you profess it: and he shun'd not the Combat
For fear or doubt of these: blush and repent,
That you in thought e're did that wrong to valour.

Beaup. Why, this is rare.

Cham. 'Fore heaven, exceeding rare;
Why modest Lady, you that sing such Encomiums
Of your first Suiter—

Verd. How can ye convince us
In your reports?

Lam. With what you cannot answer,
'Twas my command that staid him.

Cham. Your command?

Lam. Mine, Sir, and had my will rank'd with my power,
And his obedience, I could have sent him
With more ease, weaponless to you, and bound,
Than have kept him back, so well he loves his honour
Beyond his life.

Cham. Better, and better still.

Lam. I wrought with him in private to divert him
From your assur'd destruction, had he met you.

Cham. In private?

Lam. Yes, and us'd all Arts, all Charms
Of one that knew her self the absolute Mistris
Of all his faculties.

Cham. Gave all rewards too
His service could deserve; did not he take
The measure of my sheets?

Lam. Do not look yellow,
I have cause to speak; frowns cannot fright me,
By all my hopes, as I am spotless to you,
If I rest once assur'd you do but doubt me,
Or curb me of that freedom you once gave me—

Cham. What then?

Lam. I'le not alone abuse your bed, that's nothing,
But to your more vexation, 'tis resolv'd on,
I'le run away, and then try if *Dinant*
Have courage to defend me.

Champ. Impudent!

Verd. And on the sudden—

Beau. How are ye transform'd
From what you were?

42

Lam. I was an innocent Virgin,
And I can truly swear, a Wife as pure
As ever lay by Husband, and will dy so,
Let me live unsuspected, I am no servant,
Nor will be us'd like one: If you desire
To keep me constant as I would be, let
Trust and belief in you beget and nurse it;
Unnecessary jealousies make more whores
Than all baits else laid to entrap our frailties.

Beau. There's no contesting with her, from a child
Once mov'd, she hardly was to be appeas'd,
Yet I dare swear her honest.

Cham. So I think too,
On better judgement: I am no Italian
To lock her up; nor would I be a Dutchman,
To have my Wife, my soveraign, to command me:
I'le try the gentler way, but if that fail,
Believe it, Sir, there's nothing but extreams
Which she must feel from me.

Beau. That, as you please, Sir.

Charl. You have won the breeches, Madam, look up sweetly,
My Lord limps toward you.

Lam. You will learn more manners.

Charl. This is a fee, for counsel that's unask'd for.

Cham. Come, I mistook thee sweet, prethee forgive me,
I never will be jealous: e're I cherish
Such a mechanick humour, I'le be nothing;
I'le say, *Dinant* is all that thou wouldst have him,
Will that suffice?

Lam. 'Tis well, Sir.

Cham. Use thy freedom
Uncheck'd, and unobserv'd, if thou wilt have it,
These shall forget their honour, I my wrongs.
We'll all dote on him, hell be my reward

If I dissemble.

Lam. And that hell take me
If I affect him, he's a lustfull villain,
(But yet no coward) and sollicites me
To my dishonour, that's indeed a quarrel,
And truly mine, which I will so revenge,
As it shall fright such as dare only think
To be adulterers.

Cham. Use thine own waies,
I give up all to thee.

Beau. O women, women!
When you are pleas'd you are the least of evils.

Verd. I'le rime to't, but provokt, the worst of Devils.   [*Exeunt.*

    Enter Monsieur Sampson, *and three Clients.*

Samp. I know Monsieur *La-writ.*

1 Cly. Would he knew himself, Sir.

Samp. He was a pretty Lawyer, a kind of pretty Lawyer,
Of a kind of unable thing.

2 Cly. A fine Lawyer, Sir,
And would have firk'd you up a business,
And out of this Court into that.

Samp. Ye are too forward
Not so fine my friends, something he could have done,
But short short.

1 Cly. I know your worships favour,
You are Nephew to the Judge, Sir.

Samp. It may be so,
And something may be done, without trotting i'th' dirt, friends;
It may be I can take him in his Chamber,
And have an hours talk, it may be so,
And tell him that in's ear; there are such courtesies;

I will not say, I can.

3 *Cly.* We know you can, Sir.

Sam. Peradventure I, peradventure no: but where's *La-writ*?
Where's your sufficient Lawyer?

1 *Cly.* He's blown up, Sir.

2 *Cly.* Run mad and quarrels with the Dog he meets;
He is no Lawyer of this world now.

Sam. Your reason?
Is he defunct? is he dead?

2 *Cly.* No he's not dead yet, Sir;
But I would be loth to take a lease on's life for two hours:
Alas, he is possest Sir, with the spirit of fighting
And quarrels with all people; but how he came to it —

Samp. If he fight well and like a Gentleman,
The man may fight, for 'tis a lawfull calling.
Look you my friends, I am a civil Gentleman,
And my Lord my Uncle loves me.

3 *Cly.* We all know it, Sir.

Sam. I think he does, Sir, I have business too, much business,
Turn you some forty or fifty Causes in a week;
Yet when I get an hour of vacancie,
I can fight too my friends, a little does well,
I would be loth to learn to fight.

1 *Cly.* But and't please you Sir,
His fighting has neglected all our business,
We are undone, our causes cast away, Sir,
His not appearance.

Sam. There he fought too long,
A little and fight well, he fought too long indeed friends;
But ne'r the less things must be as they may,
And there be wayes —

1 Cly. We know, Sir, if you please—

Sam. Something I'le do: goe rally up your Causes.

   Enter La-writ, *and a* Gentleman, *at the door.*

2 Cly. Now you may behold Sir,
And be a witness, whether we lie or no.

La-writ. I'le meet you at the Ordinary, sweet Gentlemen,
And if there be a wench or two—

Gen. We'll have 'em.

La-writ. No handling any Duells before I come,
We'll have no going else, I hate a coward.

Gent. There shall be nothing done.

La-writ. Make all the quarrels
You can devise before I come, and let's all fight,
There is no sport else.

Gent. We'll see what may be done, Sir.

1 Cly. Ha? Monsieur *La-writ.*

La-writ. Baffled in way of business,
My causes cast away, Judgement against us?
Why there it goes.

2 Cly. What shall we do the whilst Sir?

La-wr. Breed new dissentions, goe hang your selves
'Tis all one to me; I have a new trade of living.

1 Cli. Do you hear what he saies Sir?

Sam. The Gentleman speaks finely.

La-wr. Will any of you fight? Fighting's my occupation
If you find your selves aggriev'd.

Sam. A compleat Gentleman.

La-writ. Avant thou buckram budget of petitions,
Thou spittle of lame causes; I lament for thee,
And till revenge be taken—

Sam. 'Tis most excellent.

La-wr. There, every man chuse his paper, and his place.
I'le answer ye all, I will neglect no mans business
But he shall have satisfaction like a Gentleman,
The Judge may do and not do, he's but a Monsieur.

Sam. You have nothing of mine in your bag, Sir.

La-writ. I know not Sir,
But you may put any thing in, any fighting thing.

Sam. It is sufficient, you may hear hereafter.

La-writ. I rest your servant Sir.

Sam. No more words Gentlemen
But follow me, no more words as you love me,
The Gentleman's a noble Gentleman.
I shall do what I can, and then—

Cli. We thank you Sir.   [*Ex.* Sam. *and* Clients.

Sam. Not a word to disturb him, he's a Gentleman.

La-writ. No cause go o' my side? the judge cast all?
And because I was honourably employed in action,
And not appear'd, pronounce? 'tis very well,
'Tis well faith, 'tis well, Judge.

    Enter Cleremont.

Cler. Who have we here?
My little furious Lawyer?

La-writ. I say 'tis well,
But mark the end.

Cler. How he is metamorphos'd!
Nothing of Lawyer left, not a bit of buckram,
No solliciting face now,
This is no simple conversion.
Your servant Sir, and Friend.

La-writ. You come in time, Sir,

Cler. The happier man, to be at your command then.

La-writ. You may wonder to see me thus; but that's all one,
Time shall declare; 'tis true I was a Lawyer,
But I have mew'd that coat, I hate a Lawyer,
I talk'd much in the Court, now I hate talking,
I did you the office of a man.

Cler. I must confess it.

La-w. And budg'd not, no I budg'd not.

Cler. No, you did not.

La-w. There's it then, one good turn requires another.

Cler. Most willing Sir, I am ready at your service.

La-w. There, read, and understand, and then deliver it.

Cler. This is a Challenge, Sir,

La-w. 'Tis very like, Sir,
I seldom now write Sonnets.

Cler. O admirantis,
To Monsieur *Vertaign,* the President.

La-w. I chuse no Fool, Sir.

Cler. Why, he's no Sword-man, Sir.

La-w. Let him learn, let him learn,
Time, that trains Chickens up, will teach him quickly.

Cler. Why, he's a Judge, an Old Man.

La-w. Never too Old
To be a Gentleman; and he that is a Judge
Can judge best what belongs to wounded honour.
There are my griefs, he has cast away my causes,
In which he has bowed my reputation.
And therefore Judge, or no Judge.

Cler. 'Pray be rul'd Sir,
This is the maddest thing —

La-w. You will not carry it.

Cler. I do not tell you so, but if you may be perswaded.

La-w. You know how you us'd me when I would not fight,
Do you remember, Gentleman?

Cler. The Devil's in him.

La-w. I see it in your Eyes, that you dare do it,
You have a carrying face, and you shall carry it.

Cler. The least is Banishment.

La-w. Be banish'd then;
'Tis a friends part, we'll meet in *Africa*,
Or any part of the Earth.

Cler. Say he will not fight.

La-w. I know then what to say, take you no care, Sir,

Cler. Well, I will carry it, and deliver it,
And to morrow morning meet you in the Louver,
Till when, my service.

La-w. A Judge, or no Judge, no Judge.   [*Exit* La-writ.

Cler. This is the prettiest Rogue that e'r I read of,
None to provoke to th' field, but the old President;
What face shall I put on? if I come in earnest,

49

I am sure to wear a pair of Bracelets;
This may make some sport yet, I will deliver it,
Here comes the President.

    Enter Vertaign, *with two Gentlemen.*

Vert. I shall find time, Gentlemen,
To do your causes good, is not that *Cleremont*?

1 Gent. 'Tis he my Lord.

Vert. Why does he smile upon me?
Am I become ridiculous? has your fortune, Sir,
Upon my Son, made you contemn his Father?
The glory of a Gentleman is fair bearing.

Cler. Mistake me not my Lord, you shall not find that,
I come with no blown Spirit to abuse you,
I know your place and honour due unto it,
The reverence to your silver Age and Vertue.

Vert. Your face is merry still.

Cler. So is my business,
And I beseech your honour mistake me not,
I have brought you from a wild or rather Mad-man
As mad a piece of—you were wont to love mirth
In your young days, I have known your Honour woo it,
This may be made no little one, 'tis a Challenge, Sir,
Nay, start not, I beseech you, it means you no harm,
Nor any Man of Honour, or Understanding,
'Tis to steal from your serious hours a little laughter;
I am bold to bring it to your Lordship.

Vert. 'Tis to me indeed:
Do they take me for a Sword-man at these years?

Cler. 'Tis only worth your Honours Mirth, that's all Sir,
'Thad been in me else a sawcy rudeness.

Vert. From one *La-writ*, a very punctual Challenge.

Cler. But if your Lordship mark it, no great matter.

Vert. I have known such a wrangling Advocate,
Such a little figent thing; Oh I remember him,
A notable talking Knave, now out upon him,
Has challeng'd me downright, defied me mortally
I do remember too, I cast his Causes.

Cler. Why, there's the quarrel, Sir, the mortal quarrel.

Vert. Why, what a Knave is this? as y'are a Gentleman,
Is there no further purpose but meer mirth?
What a bold Man of War! he invites me roundly.

Cler. If there should be, I were no Gentleman,
Nor worthy of the honour of my Kindred.
And though I am sure your Lordship hates my Person,
Which Time may bring again into your favour,
Yet for the manners—

Vert. I am satisfied,
You see, Sir, I have out-liv'd those days of fighting,
And therefore cannot do him the honour to beat him my self;
But I have a Kinsman much of his ability,
His Wit and Courage, for this call him Fool,
One that will spit as senseless fire as this Fellow.

Cler. And such a man to undertake, my Lord?

Vert. Nay he's too forward; these two pitch Barrels together.

Cler. Upon my soul, no harm.

Vert. It makes me smile,
Why, what a stinking smother will they utter!
Yes, he shall undertake, Sir, as my Champion,
Since you propound it mirth, I'll venture on it,
And shall defend my cause, but as y'are honest
Sport not with bloud.

Cler. Think not so basely, good Sir.

Vert. A Squire shall wait upon you from my Kinsman,
To morrow morning make you sport at full,
You want no Subject; but no wounds.

Cler. That's my care.

Ver. And so good day.   [*Ex.* Vertaign, *and Gentlemen.*

Cler. Many unto your honour.
This is a noble Fellow, of a sweet Spirit,
Now must I think how to contrive this matter,
For together they shall go.

  Enter Dinant.

Din. O *Cleremont,*
I am glad I have found thee.

Cler. I can tell thee rare things.

Din. O, I can tell thee rarer,
Dost thou love me?

Cler. Love thee?

Din. Dost thou love me dearly?
Dar'st thou for my sake?

Cler. Any thing that's honest.

Din. Though it be dangerous?

Cler. Pox o' dangerous.

Din. Nay wondrous dangerous.

Cler. Wilt thou break my heart?

Din. Along with me then.

Cler. I must part to morrow.

Din. You shall, you shall, be faithful for this night,
And thou hast made thy friend.

Cler. Away, and talk not.   [*Exeunt.*

Enter Lamira, *and Nurse.*

Lam. O Nurse, welcome, where's *Dinant?*

Nurse. He's at my back.
'Tis the most liberal Gentleman, this Gold
He gave me for my pains, nor can I blame you,
If you yield up the fort.

Lam. How? yield it up?

Nurse. I know not, he that loves, and gives so largely,
And a young Lord to boot, or I am cozen'd,
May enter every where.

Lam. Thou'lt make me angry.

Enter Dinant, *and* Cleremont.

Nur. Why, if you are, I hope here's one will please you,
Look on him with my Eyes, good luck go with you:
Were I young for your sake —

Din. I thank thee, Nurse.

Nur. I would be tractable, and as I am —

Lam. Leave the room,
So old, and so immodest! and be careful,
Since whispers will 'wake sleeping jealousies,
That none disturb my Lord.   [*Exit Nurse.*

Cler. Will you dispatch?
Till you come to the matter be not rapt thus,
Walk in, walk in, I am your scout for once,
You owe me the like service.

Din. And will pay it.

Lam. As you respect our lives, speak not so loud.

Cler. Why, do it in dumb shew then, I am silenc'd.

Lam. Be not so hasty, Sir, the golden Apples
Had a fell Dragon for their Guard, your pleasures
Are to be attempted with *Herculean* danger,
Or never to be gotten.

Din. Speak the means.

Lam. Thus briefly, my Lord sleeps now, and alas,
Each Night, he only sleeps.

Cler. Go, keep her stirring.

Lam. Now if he 'wake, as sometimes he does,
He only stretches out his hand and feels,
Whether I am a bed, which being assur'd of,
He sleeps again; but should he miss me, Valour
Could not defend our lives.

Din. What's to be done then?

Lam. Servants have servile faiths, nor have I any
That I dare trust; on noble *Cleremont*
We safely may rely.

Cler. What man can do,
Command and boldly.

Lam. Thus then in my place,
You must lye with my Lord.

Cler. With an old man?
Two Beards together, that's preposterous.

Lam. There is no other way, and though 'tis dangerous,
He having servants within call, and arm'd too,
Slaves fed to act all that his jealousie
And rage commands them, yet a true friend should not
Check at the hazard of a life.

Cler. I thank you,
I love my friend, but know no reason why
To hate my self; to be a kind of pander,
You see I am willing,

But to betray mine own throat you must pardon.

Din. Then I am lost, and all my hopes defeated,
Were I to hazard ten times more for you,
You should find, *Cleremont* —

Cler. You shall not outdo me,
Fall what may fall, I'll do't.

Din. But for his Beard —

Lam. To cover that you shall have my night Linnen,
And you dispos'd of, my *Dinant* and I
Will have some private conference.

    Enter Champernel, *privately.*

Cler. Private doing,
Or I'll not venture.

Lam. That's as we agree.   [*Exeunt.*

    Enter Nurse, and Charlotte, *pass over the Stage with Pillows, Night cloaths, and such things.*

Cham. What can this Woman do, preserving her honour?
I have given her all the liberty that may be,
I will not be far off though, nor I will not be jealous,
Nor trust too much, I think she is vertuous,
Yet when I hold her best, she's but a Woman,
As full of frailty as of faith, a poor sleight Woman,
And her best thoughts, but weak fortifications,
There may be a Mine wrought: Well, let 'em work then,
I shall meet with it, till the signs be monstrous,
And stick upon my head, I will not believe it,   [*Stands private.*
She may be, and she may not, now to my observation.

    Enter Dinant, *and* Lamira.

Din. Why do you make me stay so? if you love me —

Lam. You are too hot and violent.

Din. Why do you shift thus
From one Chamber to another?

Lam. A little delay, Sir,
Like fire, a little sprinkled o'r with water
Makes the desires burn clear, and ten times hotter.

Din. Why do you speak so loud? I pray'e go in,
Sweet Mistriss, I am mad, time steals away,
And when we would enjoy—

Lam. Now fie, fie, Servant,
Like sensual Beasts shall we enjoy our pleasures?

Din. 'Pray do not kiss me then.

Lam. Why, that I will, and you shall find anon, servant.

Din. Softly, for heavens sake, you know my friend's engag'd,
A little now, now; will ye go in again?

Lam. Ha, ha, ha, ha.

Din. Why do you laugh so loud, Precious?
Will you betray me; ha' my friends throat cut?

Lam. Come, come, I'll kiss thee again.

Cham. Will you so? you are liberal,
If you do cozen me—

Enter Nurse with Wine.

Din. What's this?

Lam. Wine, Wine, a draught or two.

Din. What does this Woman here?

Lam. She shall not hinder you.

Din. This might have been spar'd,
'Tis but delay and time lost; pray send her softly off.

Lam. Sit down, and mix your spirits with Wine,
I will make you another *Hercules.*

Din. I dare not drink;
Fie, what delays you make! I dare not,
I shall be drunk presently, and do strange things then.

Lam. Not drink a cup with your Mistriss! O the pleasure.

Din. Lady, why this?   [*Musick.*

Lam. We must have mirth to our Wine, Man.

Din. Pl— — o' the Musick.

Champ. God-a-mercy Wench,
If thou dost cuckold me I shall forgive thee.

Din. The house will all rise now, this will disturb all.
Did you do this?

Lam. Peace, and sit quiet, fool,
You love me, come, sit down and drink.

    Enter Cleremont *above.*

Cler. What a Devil ail you?
How cold I sweat! a hogs pox stop your pipes,   [*Musick.*
The thing will 'wake; now, now, methinks I find
His Sword just gliding through my throat. What's that?
A vengeance choak your pipes. Are you there, Lady?
Stop, stop those Rascals; do you bring me hither
To be cut into minced meat? why *Dinant*?

Din. I cannot do withal;
I have spoke, and spoke; I am betray'd and lost too.

Cler. Do you hear me? do you understand me?
'Plague dam your Whistles.   [*Musick ends.*

Lam. 'Twas but an over-sight, they have done, lye down.

Cler. Would you had done too,

You know not
In what a misery and fear I lye.
You have a Lady in your arms.

Din. I would have—   [*The Recorders again.*

Champ. I'll watch you Goodman Wou'd have.

Cler. Remove for Heavens sake,
And fall to that you come for.

Lam. Lie you down,
'Tis but an hours endurance now.

Cler. I dare not, softly sweet Lady — —heart?

Lam. 'Tis nothing but your fear, he sleeps still soundly,
Lie gently down.

Cler. 'Pray make an end.

Din. Come, Madam.

Lam. These Chambers are too near.   [*Ex.* Din. Lam.

Cham. I shall be nearer;
Well, go thy wayes, I'le trust thee through the world,
Deal how thou wilt: that that I never feel,
I'le never fear. Yet by the honour of a Souldier,
I hold thee truly noble: How these things will look,
And how their blood will curdle! Play on Children,
You shall have pap anon. O thou grand Fool,
That thou knew'st but thy fortune—   [*Musick done.*

Cler. Peace, good Madam,
Stop her mouth, *Dinant*, it sleeps yet, 'pray be wary,
Dispatch, I cannot endure this misery,
I can hear nothing more; I'll say my prayers,
And down again—   [*Whistle within.*
A thousand Alarms fall upon my quarters,
Heaven send me off; when I lye keeping Courses.
Pl— — o' your fumbling, *Dinant*; how I shake!
'Tis still again: would I were in the *Indies*.   [*Exit* Cler.

Enter Dinant, *and* Lamira: *a light within.*

Din. Why do you use me thus? thus poorly? basely?
Work me into a hope, and then destroy me?
Why did you send for me? this new way train me?

Lam. Mad-man, and fool, and false man, now I'll shew thee.

Din. 'Pray put your light out.

Lam. Nay I'll hold it thus,
That all chaste Eyes may see thy lust, and scorn it.
Tell me but this when you first doted on me,
And made suit to enjoy me as your Wife,
Did you not hold me honest?

Din. Yes, most vertuous.

Lam. And did not that appear the only lustre
That made me worth your love and admiration?

Din. I must confess—

Lam. Why would you deal so basely?
So like a thief, a Villain?

Din. Peace, good Madam.

Lam. I'll speak aloud too; thus maliciously,
Thus breaking all the Rules of honesty,
Of honour and of truth, for which I lov'd you,
For which I call'd you servant, and admir'd you;
To steal that Jewel purchas'd by another,
Piously set in Wedlock, even that Jewel,
Because it had no flaw, you held unvaluable:
Can he that has lov'd good, dote on the Devil?
For he that seeks a Whore, seeks but his Agent;
Or am I of so wild and low a blood?
So nurs'd in infamies?

Din. I do not think so,
And I repent.

Lam. That will not serve your turn, Sir.

Din. It was your treaty drew me on.

Lam. But it was your villany
Made you pursue it; I drew you but to try
How much a man, and nobly thou durst stand,
How well you had deserv'd the name of vertuous;
But you like a wild torrent, mix'd with all
Beastly and base affections came floating on,
Swelling your poyson'd billows—

Din. Will you betray me?

Lam. To all the miseries a vext Woman may.

Din. Let me but out,
Give me but room to toss my Sword about me,
And I will tell you y'are a treacherous woman,
O that I had but words!

Lam. They will not serve you.

Din. But two-edg'd words to cut thee; a Lady traytor?
Perish by a proud Puppet? I did you too much honour,
To tender you my love, too much respected you
To think you worthy of my worst embraces.
Go take your Groom, and let him dally with you,
Your greasie Groom; I scorn to imp your lame stock,
You are not fair, nor handsome, I lyed loudly,
This tongue abus'd you when it spoke you beauteous.

Lam. 'Tis very well, 'tis brave.

Din. Put out your light,
Your lascivious eyes are flames enough
For Fools to find you out; a Lady Plotter!
Must I begin your sacrifice of mischief?
I and my friend, the first-fruits of that bloud,
You and your honourable Husband aim at?
Crooked and wretched you are both.

Lam. To you, Sir,

Yet to the Eye of Justice straight as Truth.

Din. Is this a womans love? a womans mercy?
Do you profess this seriously? do you laugh at me?

Lam. Ha, ha.

Din. Pl——light upon your scorns, upon your flatteries,
Upon your tempting faces, all destructions;
A bedrid winter hang upon your cheeks,
And blast, blast, blast those buds of Pride that paint you;
Death in your eyes to fright men from these dangers:
Raise up your trophy, *Cleremont.*

Cler. What a vengeance ail you?

Din. What dismal noise! is there no honour in you?
Cleremont, we are betrayed, betrayed, sold by a woman;
Deal bravely for thy self.

Cler. This comes of rutting;
Are we made stales to one another?

Din. Yes, we are undone, lost.

Cler. You shall pay for't grey-beard.
Up, up, you sleep your last else.   {*Lights above, two Servants*
                    {*and* Anabel.
1 Serv. No, not yet, Sir,
Lady, look up, would you have wrong'd this Beauty?
Wake so tender a Virgin with rough terms?
You wear a Sword, we must entreat you leave it.

2 Serv. Fye Sir, so sweet a Lady?

Cler. Was this my bed-fellow, pray give me leave to look,
I am not mad yet, I may be by and by.
Did this lye by me?
Did I fear this? is this a Cause to shake at?
Away with me for shame, I am a Rascal.

Enter Champernel, Beaupre, Verdone, Lamira, Anabel, Cleremont, *and two Servants.*

Din. I am amaz'd too.

Beaup. We'll recover you.

Verd. You walk like *Robin-good-fellow* all the house over,
And every man afraid of you.

Din. 'Tis well, Lady;
The honour of this deed will be your own,
The world shall know your bounty.

Beaup. What shall we do with 'em?

Cler. Geld me,
For 'tis not fit I should be a man again,
I am an Ass, a Dog.

Lam. Take your revenges,
You know my Husbands wrongs and your own losses.

Anab. A brave man, an admirable brave man;
Well, well, I would not be so tryed again;
A very handsome proper Gentleman.

Cler. Will you let me lye by her but one hour more,
And then hang me?

Din. We wait your malice, put your swords home bravely,
You have reason to seek bloud.

Lam. Not as you are noble.

Cham. Hands off, and give them liberty, only disarm 'em.

Beaup. We have done that already.

Cham. You are welcome, Gentlemen,
I am glad my house has any pleasure for you,
I keep a couple of Ladies here, they say fair,
And you are young and handsome, Gentlemen;

Have you any more mind to Wenches?

Cler. To be abus'd too? Lady, you might have help'd this.

Ana. Sir now 'tis past, but 't may be I may stand
Your friend hereafter, in a greater matter.

Cler. Never whilst you live.

Ana. You cannot tell—now, Sir, a parting hand.

Cler. Down and Roses:
Well I may live to see you again. A dull Rogue,
No revelation in thee.

Lam. Were you well frighted?
Were your fitts from the heart, of all colds and colours?
That's all your punishment.

Cler. It might have been all yours,
Had not a block-head undertaken it.

Cham. Your swords you must leave to these Gentlemen.

Verd. And now, when you dare fight,
We are on even Ice again.

Din. 'Tis well:
To be a Mistris, is to be a monster,
And so I leave your house, and you for ever.

Lam. Leave your wild lusts, and then you are a master.

Cham. You may depart too.

Cler. I had rather stay here.

Cham. Faith we shall fright you worse.

Cler. Not in that manner,
There's five hundred Crowns, fright me but so again.

Din. Come *Cleremont*, this is the hour of fool.

Cler. Wiser the next shall be or we'll to School.   [*Exeunt.*

Champ. How coolly these hot gallants are departed!
Faith Cousin, 'twas unconscionably done,
To lye so still, and so long.

Anab. 'Twas your pleasure,
If 'twere a fault, I may hereafter mend.

Champ. O my best Wife,
Take now what course thou wilt, and lead what life.

Lam. The more trust you commit, the more care still,
Goodness and vertue shall attend my will.

Cham. Let's laugh this night out now, and count our gains.
We have our honours home, and they their pains.   [*Exeunt omnes.*

Actus Quartus. Scena Prima.

Enter Cleremont, Dinant.

Din. It holds, they will go thither.

Cler. To their Summer-house?

Din. Thither i'th' evening, and which is the most infliction,
Only to insult upon our miseries.

Cler. Are you provided?

Din. Yes, yes.

Cler. Throughly?

Din. Throughly.

Cler. Basta, enough, I have your mind, I will not fail you.

Din. At such an hour.

Cler. Have I a memory?
A Cause, and Will to do? thou art so sullen—

Din. And shall be, till I have a fair reparation.

Cler. I have more reason, for I scaped a fortune,
Which if I come so near again: I say nothing,
But if I sweat not in another fashion—
O, a delicate Wench.

Din. 'Tis certain a most handsome one.

Cler. And me thought the thing was angry with it self too
It lay so long conceal'd, but I must part with you,
I have a scene of mirth, to drive this from my heart,
And my hour is come.

Din. Miss not your time.

The Little French Lawyer

The Little French Lawyer

Cler. I dare not.   [*Exeunt severally.*

  Enter Sampson, *and a Gentleman.*

Gent. I presume, Sir, you now need no instruction,
But fairly know, what belongs to a Gentleman;
You bear your Uncles cause.

Sam. Do not disturb me,
I understand my cause, and the right carriage.

Gent. Be not too bloody.

Sam. As I find my enemy; if his sword bite,
If it bite, Sir, you must pardon me.

Gent. No doubt he is valiant,
He durst not undertake else,

Sam. He's most welcome,
As he is most valiant, he were no man for me else.

Gent. But say he should relent.

Sam. He dies relenting,
I cannot help it, he must di[e] relenting,
If he pray, praying, *ipso facto*, praying,
Your honourable way admits no prayer,
And if he fight, he falls, there's his *quietus*.

Gent. Y'are nobly punctual, let's retire and meet 'em,
But still, I say, have mercy.

Samp. I say, honour.   [*Exeunt.*

  Enter Champernel, Lamira, Anabel, Beaupre, Verdone,   Charlote
and a Servant.

Lam. Will not you go sweet-heart?

Champ. Go? I'le fly with thee.
I stay behind?

Lam. My Father will be there too,
And all our best friends.

Beau. And if we be not merry,
We have hard luck, Lady.

Verd. Faith let's have a kind of play.

Cham. What shall it be?

Verd. The story of *Dinant*.

Lam. With the merry conceits of *Cleremont*,
His Fits and Feavers.

Ana. But I'le lie still no more.

Lam. That, as you make the Play, 'twill be rare sport,
And how 'twill vex my gallants, when they hear it!
Have you given order for the Coach?

Charl. Yes, Madam.

Cham. My easie Nag, and padd.

Serv. 'Tis making ready.

Champ. Where are your Horses?

Beau. Ready at an hour, Sir: we'll not be last.

Cham. Fie, what a night shall we have!
A roaring, merry night.

Lam. We'll flie at all, Sir.

Cham. I'le flie at thee too, finely, and so ruffle thee,
I'le try your Art upon a Country pallet.

Lam. Brag not too much, for fear I should expect it,
Then if you fail—

Cham. Thou saiest too true, we all talk.

But let's in, and prepare, and after dinner
Begin our mirthful pilgrimage.

Lam. He that's sad,
A crab-face'd Mistris cleave to him for this year.   [*Exeunt.*

   Enter Cleremont, *and* La-writ.

La-writ. Since it cannot be the Judge—

Cler. 'Tis a great deal better.

La-writ. You are sure, he is his kinsman? a Gentleman?

Cler. As arrant a Gentleman, and a brave fellow,
And so near to his blood—

La-writ. It shall suffice,
I'le set him further off, I'le give a remove
Shall quit his kindred, I'le lopp him.

Cl[e]r. Will ye kill him?

La-w. And there were no more Cousins in the world I kill him,
I do mean, Sir, to kill all my Lords kindred.
For every cause a Cousin.

Cler. How if he have no more Cousins?

La-writ. The next a kin then to his Lordships favour;
The man he smiles upon.

Cler. Why this is vengeance, horrid, and dire.

La-writ. I love a dire revenge:
Give me the man that will all others kill,
And last himself,

Cler. You stole that resolution.

La-writ. I had it in a Play, but that's all one,
I wou'd see it done.

Cler. Come, you must be more merciful.

La-writ. To no Lords Cousins in the world, I hate 'em;
A Lords Cousin to me is a kind of Cockatrice,
If I see him first, he dies.
A strange Antipathy.

Cler. What think you of their Nieces?

La-writ. If I like 'em,
They may live, and multiply; 'tis a cold morning.

Cler. 'Tis sharp indeed; you have broke your fast?

La-writ. No verily.

Cler. Your valour would have ask'd a good foundation.

La-writ. Hang him, I'le kill him fasting.

   Enter Sampson *and the Gent.*

Cler. Here they come,
Bear your self in your language, smooth and gently,
When your swords argue.

La-writ. 'Pray Sir, spare your precepts.

Gent. I have brought you, Sir —

La-writ. 'Tis very well, no words,
You are welcome, Sir.

Sam. I thank you, Sir, few words.

La-writ. I'le kill you for your Uncles sake.

Sam. I love you,
I'le cut your throat for your own sake.

La-writ. I esteem of you.

Cler. Let's render 'em honest, and fair, Gentlemen,

Search my friend, I'le search yours.

Gent. That's quickly done.

Cler. You come with no Spells, nor Witchcrafts?

Sam. I come fairly to kill him honestly.

La-writ. Hang Spells, and Witchcrafts,
I come to kill my Lords Nephew like a Gentleman,
And so I kiss his hand.

Gent. This Doublet is too stiff.

La-writ. Off with't, I hate it,
And all such fortifications, feel my skin,
If that be stiff, flea that off too.

Gent. 'Tis no soft one.

La-writ. Off with't, I say:
I'le fight with him like a flea'd Cat.

Gent. You are well, you are well.

Cler. You must uncase too.

Sam. Yes, Sir.
But tell me this, why should I mix mine honour
With a fellow, that has ne're a lace in's shirt?

Gent. That's a main point, my friend has two.

Cler. That's true, Sir.

La-w. Base and degenerate Cousin, dost not thou know
An old, and tatter'd colours, to the enemy,
Is of more honour, and shews more ominous?
This shirt, five times, victorious I have fought under,
And cut through squadrons of your curious cut-works,
As I will do through thine, shake, and be satisfied.

Cler. This is unanswerable.

Sam. But may I fight with a foul shirt?

Gent. Most certain, so it be a fighting shirt,
Let it be ne're so foul, or lowsie, *Cæsar* wore such a one.

Sam. Saint *Denis* then: I accept your shirt.

Cler. Not so forward, first you must talk,
'Tis a main point, of the French method,
Talk civilly, and make your cause Authentick.

Gent. No weapon must be near you, nor no anger.

Cler. When you have done, then stir your resolutions,
Take to your Weapons bravely.

La-writ. 'Tis too cold;
This for a Summer fight.

Cler. Not for a world you should transgress the rules.

Sam. 'Tis pievish weather,
I had rather fight without.

Gent. An 'twere in a River.

Cler. Where both stood up to th' chins.

La-writ. Then let's talk quickly,
Pl— — o' this circumstance.

Cler. Are the Horses come yet?

Gent. Yes certain: give your swords to us, now civilly.

Cler. We'll stand a while off; take the things, and leave 'em,
You know when, and let the children play:
This is a dainty time of year for puppies,
Would the old Lord were here.

Gent. He would dye with laughter.

Cler. I am sorry I have no time to see this game out,

Away, away.

Gent. Here's like to be a hot fight,
Call when y'are fit.   [*Ex.* Cler. *and Gent.*

La-writ. Why look you Sir, you seem to be a Gentleman,
And you come in honour of your Uncle, boh, boh, 'tis very cold;
Your Uncle has offer'd me some few affronts,
Past flesh and blood to bear: boh, boh, wondrous cold.

Sam. My Lord, mine Uncle, is an honourable man,
And what he offers, boh, boh, cold indeed,
Having made choice of me, an unworthy kinsman,
Yet take me with you: boh, boh, pestilence cold,
Not altogether.

La-writ. Boh, boh, I say altogether.

Sam. You say you know not what then? boh, boh, Sir.

La-writ. Sir me with your sword in your hand;
You have a scurvy Uncle, you have a most scurvy cause,
And you are—boh, boh.

Sam. Boh, boh, what?

La-writ. A shitten scurvy Cousin.

Samp. Our Swords; our Swords;
Thou art a Dog, and like a Dog, our Swords.

La-w. Our weapons Gentlemen: ha? where's your second?

Sam. Where's yours?

La-writ. So ho; our weapons.

Sam. Wa, ha, ho, our weapons;
Our Doublets and our weapons, I am dead.

La-w. First, second, third, a pl— — be wi' you Gentlemen.

Sam. Are these the rules of honour? I am starv'd.

La-w. They are gone, and we are here; what shall we do?

Sam. O for a couple of Faggots.

La-w. Hang a couple of Faggots.
Dar'st thou take a killing cold with me?

Sam. I have it already.

La-w. Rogues, Thieves, boh, boh, run away with our Doublets?
To fight at Buffets now, 'twere such a May-game.

Sam. There were no honour in't, pl — — on't, 'tis scurvy.

La-w. Or to revenge my wrongs at fisty-cuffes.

Sam. My Lord, mine Uncles cause, depend on Boxes?

La-w. Let's go in quest, if we ever recover 'em.

Sam. I, come, our Colds together, and our Doublets.

La-w. Give me thy hand; thou art a valiant Gentleman,
I say if ever we recover 'em —

Sam. Let's get into a house and warm our hearts.

La-w. There's ne're a house within this mile, beat me,
Kick me and beat me as I go, and I'le beat thee too,
To keep us warm; if ever we recover 'em —
Kick hard, I am frozen: so, so, now I feel it.

Sam. I am dull yet.

La-w. I'le warm thee, I'le warm thee — Gentlemen?
Rogues, Thieves, Thieves: run now I'le follow thee.   [*Exeunt.*

   Enter Vertaign, Champernel, Beaupre, Verdone, Lamira,
   Annabel, Charlotte, *Nurse.*

Verta. Use legs, and have legs.

Cham. You that have legs say so,

I put my one to too much stress.

Verdo. Your Horse, Sir,
Will meet you within half a mile.

Lam. I like
The walk so well, I should not miss my Coach,
Though it were further. *Annabel* thou art sad:
What ails my Niece?

Beau. She's still musing, Sister,
How quietly her late bed-fellow lay by her.

Nurse. Old as I am, he would have startled me,
Nor can you blame her.

Char. Had I ta'ne her place,
I know not, but I fear, I should ha' shreek'd,
Though he had never offer'd —

Ana. Out upon thee,
Thou wouldst have taught him.

Char. I think, with your pardon,
That you wish now you had.

Ana. I am glad I yield you   [*Cornet.*
Such ample scope of mirth.   [*Musick within.*

Verta. Nay, be not angry,
There's no ill meant: ha? Musick, and choice Musick?

Cham. 'Tis near us in the Grove; what courteous bounty
Bestows it on us? my dancing days are done;
Yet I would thank the giver, did I know him.

Verdo. 'Tis questionless, some one of your own Village,
That hearing of your purpos'd journey thither,
Prepares it for your entertainment, and
The honour of my Lady.

Lam. I think rather,
Some of your Lordships Clients.

Beaup. What say you Cousin,
If they should prove your Suitors?

Verd. That's most likely.

Nurse. I say if you are noble, be't who will,
Go presently and thank 'em: I can jump yet,
Or tread a measure.

Lam. Like a Millers Mare.

Nurs. I warrant you well enough to serve the Country,
I'le make one, and lead the way.   [*Exit.*

Charl. Do you note,
How zealous the old Crone is?

Lam. And you titter
As eagerly as she: come sweet, we'll follow,
No ill can be intended.   [*Musick ends.*

Cham. I ne're feared yet.   [*Exeunt.*

    SONG in the Wood.

    This way, this way come and hear,
    You that hold these pleasures dear,
    Fill your ears with our sweet sound,
    Whilst we melt the frozen ground:
    This way come, make haste oh fair,
    Let your clear eyes gild the Air;
    Come and bless us with your sight,
    This way, this way, seek delight.

    Enter company of Gentlemen, like Ruffians.

1 Gent. They are ours, but draw them on a little further
From the foot-path into the neighbouring thicket,
And we may do't, as safe as in a Castle.

2 Gent. They follow still; the President *Vertaigne*
Comes on a pace, and *Champernel* limps after;
The Women, as if they had wings, and walk't

Upon the Air, fly to us.

1 Gent. They are welcome,
We'll make 'em sport; make a stand here, all know
How we are to proceed.

2 Gent. We are instructed.　　　[*Still Musick within.*

1 Gent. One strain or two more.　　　[*Gent. off.*

　Enter Vertaigne, Champernel, Beaupre, Verdone, Lamira, Anabel, *Nurse*, Charlote.

Excellent, they are come.

Nurse. We cannot miss, in such a business, yet
Mine ear ne'r fail'd me.　　　[*Musick for the Dance.*

Charl. Would we were at it once,
I do not walk, but Dance.

1 Gent. You shall have dancing.
Begin, and when I give the word—

2 Gent. No more:
We are instructed.　　　　　　　[*Dance.*

Beaupre. But win us fairly—

1 Gent. O Sir, we do not come to try your valour,
But to possess you, yet we use you kindly
In that, like English Thieves, we kill you not,
But are contented with the spoil.

Verta. Oh Heaven!
How hath mine age deserv'd this?

Cham. Hell confound it,
This comes of walking; had I kept my legs,
Or my good Horse, my Armour on,
My Staff in my rest, and this good Sword too, friend,
How I would break and scatter these.

All Gent. Ha, ha, ha.

Cham. Do you scorn me Rogues?

Nurs. Nay, Gentlemen, kind Gentlemen,
Or honest keepers of these woods, but hear me,
Be not so rough; if you are taken with
My beauty, as it hath been worth the seeking,
Some one or two of you try me in private,
You shall not find me squeamish.

Charl. Do not kill me,
And do your worst, I'le suffer.

Lam. Peace vile creatures.

Vert. Do you know me, or my place, that you presume not
To touch my person?

1 Gent. If you are well, rest so,
Provoke not angry Wasps.

Verta. You are Wasps indeed,
Never created to yield Wax or Honey,
But for your Countries torment; yet if you are men,
(As you seem such in shape) if true born French-men,
However want compels you to these courses,
Rest satisfied with what you can take from us,
(These Ladies honours, and our liberties safe)
We freely give it.

1 Gent. You give but our own.

Verta. Look on these grey hairs, as you would be old,
Their tears, as you would have yours to find mercy
When Justice shall o'retake you.

Cham. Look on me,
Look on me Rascals, and learn of me too,
That have been in some part of your profession,
Before that most of you ere suck'd, I know it,
I have rode hard, and late too.

Verta. Take heed, Sir.

Cham. Then use me like a Brother of the Trade,
For I have been at Sea, as you on land are,
Restore my Matrimony undefil'd,
Wrong not my Neece, and for our gold or silver,
If I pursue you, hang me.

Nurs. 'Tis well offer'd,
And as I said, sweet Gentlemen, with sowre faces,
If you are high, and want some sport, or so,
(As living without action here, you may do)
Forbear their tender grissels, they are meat
Will wash away, there is no substance in it,
We that are expert in the game, and tough too,
Will hold you play.

   Enter Dinant *and* Cleremont.

1 Gent. This Hen longs to be troden.

Din. Lackey, my Horse.

Cler. This way, I heard the cries
Of distress'd Women.

2 Gent. Stand upon your guard.

Din. Who's here? my witty, scornful Lady-plot
In the hands of Ruffians?

Cler. And my fine cold virgin,
That was insensible of man, and woman?

Din. Justice too,
Without a sword to guard it self?

Cler. And valour with its hands bound?

Din. And the great Souldier dull?
Why this is strange.

Lam. Dinant as thou art noble—

78

Ana. As thou art valiant *Cleremont*—

Lam. As ever I appear'd lovely—

Ana. As you ever hope
For what I would give gladly—

Cler. Pretty conjurations.

Lam. All injuries a little laid behind you.

Ana. Shew your selves men, and help us.

Din. Though your many
And gross abuses of me should more move me
To triumph in your miseries than relieve you,—
Yet that hereafter you may know that I
The scorn'd and despis'd *Dinant*, know what does
Belong to honour, thus—

Cler. I will say little,   [*Fight.*
Speak thou for me.

Cham. 'Tis bravely fought.

Verta. Brave tempers,
To do thus for their enemies.

Cham. They are lost yet.

1 Gent. You that would rescue others, shall now feel
What they were born to.

2 Gent. Hurry them away.   [*Ex. Manent* Vert. *and* Champernel.

Cham. That I could follow them.

Verta. I only can lament my fortune, and desire of heaven
A little life for my revenge.

Cham. The Provost
Shall fire the woods, but I will find 'em out,
No cave, no rock, nor hell shall keep them from

My searching vengeance.

Enter La-writ, *and* Sampson.

La-writ. O cold! O fearfull cold! plague of all seconds.

Samp. O for a pint of burnt wine, or a sip
Of *aqua-fortis.*

Cham. The rogues have met with these two
Upon my life and rob'd 'em.

La-writ. As you are honourable Gentlemen,
Impart unto a couple of cold combatants.

Sam. My Lord, mine uncle as I live.

La-writ. Pox take him.
How that word has warm'd my mouth!

Verta. Why how now Cousin?
Why, why? and where man, have you been? at a Poulters
That you are cas'd thus like a rabbet? I could laugh now,
And I shall laugh, for all I have lost my Children,
Laugh monstrously.

Cham. What are they?

Verta. Give me leave Sir,
Laugh more and more, never leave laughing.

Cham. Why Sir?

Verta. Why 'tis such a thing I smell it Sir, I smell it,
Such a ridiculous thing, —

La-writ. Do you laugh at me my Lord?
I am very cold, but that should not be laught at.

Cham. What art thou?

La-writ. What art thou?

Sam. If he had his doublet. —
And his sword by his side, as a Gentleman ought to have.

Verta. Peace Monsieur *Sampson.*

Cham. Come hither little Gentleman.

La-writ. Base is the slave commanded: come to me.

Verta. This is the little advocate.

Cham. What advocate?

Verta. The little advocate that sent me a challenge,
I told you that my Nephew undertook it,
And what 'twas like to prove: now you see the issue.

Cham. Is this the little Lawyer?

La-writ. You have a sword Sir,
And I have none, you have a doublet too
That keeps you warm, and makes you merry.

Sam. If your Lordship knew
The nature, and the nobleness of the Gentleman,
Though he shew slight here, and at what gusts of danger
His manhood has arrived,
But that
Mens fates are foolish,
And often headlong overrun their fortunes.

La-writ. That little Lawyer would so prick his ears up,
And bite your honour by the nose.

Cham. Say you so Sir?

La-writ. So niggle about your grave shins Lord *Verta[ig]ne* too.

Sam. No more sweet Gentleman, no more of that Sir.

La-writ. I will have more, I must have more.

Verta. Out with it.

Sam. Nay he is as brave a fellow. —

Cham. Have I caught you?   [*Strikes him down.*

Verta. Do not kill him, do not kill him.

Cham. No, no, no, I will not. Do you peep again?
Down down proud heart.

Sam. O valour,
Look up brave friend, I have no means to rescue thee,
My Kingdom for a sword.

Cham. I'le sword you presently,
I'le claw your skin coat too.

Verta. Away good *Sampson*,
You go to grass else instantly.

Sam. But do not murder my brave friend.

Verta. Not one word.

Cham. If you do sirra —

Sam. Must I goe off dishonour'd?
Adversity tries valour, so I leave thee.   [*Exit.*

Cham. Are you a Lawyer Sir?

La-writ. I was, I was Sir.

Cham. Nay never look, your Lawyers pate is broken,
And your litigious blood about your ears sirra,
Why do you fight and snarle?

La-writ. I was possest.

Cham. I'le dispossess you.

Verta. Ha, ha, ha.

La-writ. Et tu Brute?

Verta. Beat him no more.

Cham. Alas Sir I must beat him,
Beat him into his business again, he will be lost else.

Verta. Then take your way.

Cham. Ly still, and doe not struggle.

La-writ. I am patient,
I never saw my blood before, it jades me,
I have no more heart now than a goose.

Cham. Why sirra, why do you leave your trade, your trade of living,
And send your challenges like thunderbolts,
To men of honour'd place?

La-writ. I understand Sir,
I never understood before your beating.

Cham. Does this work on you?

La-writ. Yes.

Cham. Do you thank me for't?

La-writ. As well as a beaten man can.

Cham. And do you promise me,
To fall close to your trade again? leave brawling?

La-writ. If you will give me leave and life.

Cham. And ask this noble man forgiveness?

La-writ. Heartily.

Cham. Rise then, and get you gone, and let me hear of you
As of an advocate new vampt; no more words,
Get you off quickly, and make no murmurs,
I shall pursue you else.

La-writ. I have done sweet Gentlemen.   [*Exit.*

Verta. But we forget our selves, our friends and Children.

Cham. We'l raise the country first, then take our fortunes. [*Exeunt.*

   Enter one Gentleman, *and* Lamira.

1 Gent. Shall I entreat for what I may command?

Lam. Think on my birth.

1 Gent. Here I am only Noble,
A King, and thou in my dominions, fool,
A subject and a slave.

Lam. Be not a Tyrant,
A ravisher of honour, gentle Sir,
And I will think ye such, and on my knees,
As to my Soveraign, pay a Subjects duty,
With prayers and tears.

1 Gent. I like this humble carriage,
I will walk by, but kneel you still and weep too,
It shews well, while I meditate on the prey,
Before I seize it.

Lam. Is there no mercie, Heaven?

   Enter second Gent. *and* Anabel.

2 Gent. Not kiss you?
I will kiss and kiss again.

Ana. Savage villain!
My Innocence be my strength, I do defie thee,
Thus scorn and spit at thee; will you come on Sir?
You are hot, there is a cooler.

2 Gent. A virago?

Ana. No, loathsome Goat, more, more, I am that Goddess,
That here with whips of steel in hell hereafter
Scourge rape and theft.

2 Gent. I'le try your deity.

Ana. My chastity, and this knife held by a Virgin,
Against thy lust, thy sword and thee a Beast,
Call on for the encounter.

2 Gent. Now what think you?   [*Throws her and taks her Knife.*
Are you a Goddess?

Ana. In me their power suffers,
That should protect the Innocent.

1 Gent. I am all fire,
And thou shall quench it, and serve my pleasures.
Come partner in the spoil and the reward,
Let us enjoy our purchase.

Lam. O *Dinant*!
O Heaven! O Husband!

Ana. O my *Cleremont*!

1 Gent. Two are our slaves they call on, bring 'em forth
As they are chain'd together, let them see
And suffer in the object.

   Enter Dinant, *and* Cleremont, *bound by the rest of the*
   Gent.

2 Gent. While we sit
And without pity hear 'em.

Cler. By my life,
I suffer more for thee than for my self.

Din. Be a man *Cleremont*, and look upon 'em
As such that not alone abus'd our service,
Fed us with hopes most bitter in digestion,
But when love fail'd, to draw on further mischief,
The baits they laid for us, were our own honours,
Which thus hath made us slaves too, worse than slaves.

2 Gent. He dies.

1 Gent. Pray hold, give him a little respite.

Din. I see you now beyond expression wretched,
The wit you brag'd of fool'd, that boasted honour,
As you believ'd compass'd with walls of brass,
To guard it sure, subject to be o'rethrown
With the least blast of lust.

Lam. A most sad truth.

Din. That confidence which was not to be shaken
In a perpetual fever, and those favours,
Which with so strong and Ceremonious duty
Your lover and a Gentleman long sought for,
Sought, sued, and kneel'd in vain for, must you yield up
To a licentious villain, that will hardly
Allow you thanks for't.

Cler. Something I must say too,
And to you pretty one, though crying one;
To be hang'd now, when these worshipful benchers please,
Though I know not their faces that condemn me,
A little startles me, but a man is nothing,
A Maidenhead is the thing, the thing all aim at;
Do not you wish now, and wish from your heart too,
When scarce sweet with my fears, I long lay by you
Those fears you and your good Aunt put upon me,
To make you sport, you had given a little hint,
A touch or so, to tell me I was mortal,
And by a mortal woman?

Ana. Pray you no more.

Cler. If I had loos'd that virgin Zone, observe me,
I would have hired the best of all our Poets
To have sung so much, and so well in the honour
Of that nights joy, that *Ovids* afternoon,
Nor his *Corinna* should again be mention'd.

Ana. I do repent, and wish I had.

Cler. That's comfort,
But now—

2 Gent. Another that will have it offer'd,
Compel it to be offer'd, shall enjoy it.

Cler. A rogue, a ruffian.

2 Gent. As you love your throat, —

1 Gent. Away with them.

Ana. O *Cleremont*!

Lam. O *Dinant*!

Din. I can but add your sorrows to my sorrows,
Your fears to my fears.

Cler. To your wishes mine,
This slave may prove unable to perform,
Till I perform the task that I was born for.

Ana. Amen, amen.

1 Gent. Drag the slaves hence, for you
A while I'le lock you up here, study all ways
You can to please me, or the deed being done,
You are but dead.

2 Gen. This strong Vault shall contain you,
There think how many for your maidenhead
Have pin'd away, and be prepar'd to lose it
With penitence.

1 Gent. No humane help can save you.

Ladyes. Help, help!

2 Gent. You cry in vain, rocks cannot hear you.

Actus Quintus. Scena Prima.

A Horrid noise of Musique within,
Enter one and opens the door, in which Lamira *and*
Anabel *were shut, they in all fear.*

Lam. O Cousin how I shake all this long night!
What frights and noises we have heard, still they encrease,
The villains put on shapes to torture us,
And to their Devils form such preparations
As if they were a hatching new dishonours,
And fatal ruine, past dull mans invention.
Goe not too far, and pray good Cousin *Anabel,*
Hark a new noise.   [*A strange Musick. Sackbut & Troop Musick.*

Ana. They are exquisite in mischief,
I will goe on, this room gives no protection,
More than the next, what's that? how sad and hollow,
The sound comes to us.   [*Thieves peeping. Louder.*

Lam. Groaning? or singing is it?

Ana. The wind I think, murmuring amongst old rooms.

Lam. Now it grows lowder, sure some sad presage
Of our foul loss—look now they peep.

Ana. Pox peep 'em.

Lam. O give them gentle language.

Ana. Give 'em rats-bane.   [*Peep above.*

Lam. Now they are above.

Ana. I would they were i'th' Center.

Lam. Thou art so foolish desperate.

Ana. Since we must lose.

Lam. Call 'em brave fellows, Gentlemen.

Ana. Call 'em rogues,
Rogues as they are, rude rogues, uncivil villains.

Lam. Look an thou woo't beware, dost thou feel the danger?

Ana. Till the danger feel me, thus will I talk still,
And worse when that comes too; they cannot eat me.
This is a punishment, upon our own prides
Most justly laid; we must abuse brave Gentlemen,
Make 'em tame fools, and hobby-horses, laugh and jear at
Such men too, and so handsom and so Noble,
That howsoe're we seem'd to carry it—
Wou'd 'twere to do again.

Lam. I do confess cousin,
I was too harsh, too foolish.

Ana. Do you feel it?
Do you find it now? take heed o'th' punishment,
We might have had two gallant Gentlemen,
Proper, young, O how it tortures me!
Two Devils now, two rascals, two and twenty—

Lam. O think not so.

Ana. Nay an we 'scape so modestly—

Lam. May we be worthy any eyes, or knowledge,
When we are used thus?

Ana. Why not? why do you cry?
Are we not women still? what were we made for?

Lam. But thus, thus basely—

Ana. 'Tis against our [w]ills,
And if there come a thousand so,—

Lam. Out on thee.

Ana. You are a fool, what we cannot resist,
Why should we grieve and blush for? there be women,
And they that bear the name of excellent women

Would give their whole estates to meet this fortune.

Lam. Hark, a new noise.   [*New sound within.*

Ana. Let 'em goe on, I fear not,
If wrangling, fighting and scratching cannot preserve me,
Why so be it Cousin; if I be ordain'd
To breed a race of rogues. —

    Enter four over the stage with Beaupre, *and* Verdone,   *bound and halters about their necks.*

Lam. They come.

Ana. Be firm,
They are welcom.

Lam. What mask of death is this? O my dear Brother.

Ana. My Couz too; why now y'are glorious villains.

Lam. O shall we lose our honours?

Ana. Let 'em goe,
When death prepares the way, they are but Pageants.
Why must these dye?

Beau. Lament your own misfortunes,
We perish happily before your ruins.

Ana. Has mischief ne'r a tongue?

1 Gent. Yes foolish woman,
Our Captains will is death.

Ana. You dare not do it.
Tell thy base boisterous Captain what I say,
Thy lawless Captain that he dares not;
Do you laugh you rogue? you pamper'd rogue?

Lam. Good Sir,
Good Cousin gently, as y'are a Gentleman, —

Ana. A Gentleman? a slave, a dog, the devils harbinger.

Lam. Sir as you had a Mother.

Ana. He a Mother?
Shame not the name of Mother, a she Bear
A bloody old wolf bitch, a woman Mother?
Looks that rude lump, as if he had a Mother?
Intreat him? hang him, do thy worst, thou dar'st not,
Thou dar'st not wrong their lives, thy Captain dares not,
They are persons of more price.

Ver. What e're we suffer
Let not your angers wrong you.

Ana. You cannot suffer,
The men that do this deed, must live i'th' moon
Free from the gripe of Justice.

Lam. Is it not better?

Ana. Is it not better? let 'em goe on like rascals
And put false faces on; they dare not do it;
Flatter such scabbs of nature?

Gent. Woman, woman
The next work is with you.

Ana. Unbind those Gentlemen,
And put their fatal fortunes on our necks.

Lam. As you have mercy do.

Ana. As you are monsters.

Lam. Fright us no more with shipwrack of our honours
Nor if there be a guilt by us committed
Let it endanger those.

Ana. I say they dare not,
There be a thousand gallouses, ye rogues,
Tortures, ye bloody rogues, wheels.

Gent. Away.

Lam. Stay.

Ana. Stay.
Stay and I'le flatter too: good sweet fac'd Gentlemen,
You excellent in honesty; O Kinsmen!
O Noble kinsmen!

Gent. Away with 'em. [*Ex.* Ver. Beaup. *and* Gent.

Ana. Stay yet.
The Devil and his lovely dam walk with you,
Come fortify your self, if they do dy,
Which all their ruggedness cannot rack into me,
They cannot find an hour more Innocent,
Nor more friends to revenge 'em.

    Enter Cleremont, *disguis'd.*

Lam. Now stand constant,
For now our tryal's come.

Cler. This beautie's mine,
Your minute moves not yet.

Lam. She sinks if Christian,
If any spark of noble heat. —

Cler. Rise Lady
And fearless rise, there's no dishonour meant you,
Do you know my tongue?

Ana. I have heard it.

Cler. Mark it better,
I am one that loves you, fairly, nobly loves you,
Look on my face?

Ana. O Sir?

Cler. No more words, softly
Hark, but hark wisely how, understand well,

Suspect not, fear not.

Ana. You have brought me comfort.

Cler. If you think me worthy of your husband,
I am no rogue nor Begger, if you dare do thus—

Ana. You are Monsieur *Cleremont*.

Cler. I am the same,
If you dare venture, speak, if not I leave you,
And leave you to the mercy of these villains
That will not wooe ye much.

Ana. Save my reputation,
And free me from these slaves.

Cler. By this kiss I'le do it,
And from the least dishonour they dare aim at you,
I have a Priest too, shall be ready.

Ana. You are forward.

Lam. Is this my constant cousin? how she whispers,
Kisses and huggs the thief!

Ana. You'l offer nothing.

Cler. Till all be tyed,
Not as I am a Gentleman.

Ana. Can you relieve my Aunt too?

Cler. Not yet Mistris,
But fear nothing, all shall be well, away quickly
It must be done i'th' moment or—

Ana. I am with ye.

Cler. I'le know now who sleeps by me, keep your standing.
                    [*Ex.* Cler. *and* Anabel.

Lam. Well, go thy way, and thine own shame dwell with thee.

Is this the constancy she shew'd, the bravery?
The dear love and the life she ow'd her kinsmen?
O brave tongue, valiant glorious woman!
Is this the noble anger you arriv'd at?
Are these the thieves you scorn'd, the rogues you rail'd at?
The scabs and scums of nature? O fair modesty,
Excellent vertue, whither art thou fled?
What hand O Heaven is over us, when strong virgins
Yield to their fears, and to their fears their fortunes?
Never belief come near me more, farewel wench,
A long farewel from all that ever knew thee:
My turn is next,
I am resolv'd, it comes
But in a nobler shape, ha?

   Enter Dinant.

Din. Blesse ye Lady.

Lam. Indeed Sir, I had need of many blessings,
For all the hours I have had since I came here,
Have been so many curses. How got you liberty?
For I presume you come to comfort me.

Din. To comfort you, and love you, 'tis most true,
My bondage was as yours, as full of bitterness
And every hour my death.

Lam. Heaven was your comfort.

Din. Till the last evening, sitting full of sadness,
Wailing, sweet Mistris, your unhappy fortunes,
(Mine own I had the least care of) round about me
The Captain and the company stood gaping,
When I began the story of my love
To you fair Saint, and with so full a sorrow,
Follow'd each point, that even from those rude eyes,
That never knew what pity meant or mercy,
There stole down soft relentings: take heed Mistris,
And let not such unholy hearts outdo you,
The soft plum'd god will see again; thus taken,
As men transform'd with the strange tale I told,
They stood amaz'd, then bid me rise and live,

94

Take liberty and means to see your person,
And wisht me prosperous in your love, wish you so,
Be wise and loving Lady, shew but you so.

Lam. O Sir, are these fit hours to talk of love in?
Shall we make fools of our afflictions?
Can any thing sound sweetly in mine ears,
Where all the noise of bloody horrour is?
My Brother, and my Cousin, they are dead Sir,
Dead, basely dead, is this an age to fool in?
And I my self, I know not what I shall be,
Yet I must thank you, and if happily
You had ask'd me yesterday, when these were living,
And my fears less, I might have hearkned to you.

Din. Peace to your grief, I bind you to your word.

   Enter Cleremont, Anabel, Beaupre, Verdone, Charlote,   *Nurse, the*
two Gentlemen.

Lam. How? do you conjure?

Din. Not to raise dreadfull apparitions, Madam,
But such as you would gladly see.

Lam. My Brother, and nephew living?

Beau. And both owe their lives
To the favour of these Gentlemen.

Verd. Who deserve
Our service, and for us, your gracious thanks.

Lam. Which I give freely, and become a suitor,
To be hereafter more familiar   [*Kisse.*
With such great worth and vertue.

1 Gent. Ever think us
Your servants, Madam.

Cler. Why if thou wilt needs know
How we are freed, I will discover it,
And with laconick brevity: these Gentlemen

This night incountring with those outlaws that
Yesterday made us prisoners, and as we were
Attempted by 'em they with greater courage,
(I am sure with better fortune) not alone,
Guarded themselves, but forc'd the bloody thieves,
Being got between them, and this hellish Cave,
For safety of their lives, to fly up higher
Into the woods, all left to their possession,
This sav'd your Brother, and your nephew from
The gibbet, this redeem'd me from my Chains,
And gave my friend his liberty, this preserv'd
Your honour ready to be lost.

Din. But that
I know this for a ly, and that the thieves
And gentlemen, are the same men, by my practice
Suborn'd to this, he does deliver it
With such a constant brow, that I am doubtfull,
I should believe him too.

1 Gent. If we did well,
We are rewarded.

2 Gent. Thanks but takes away
From what was freely purpos'd.

Cler. Now by this hand,
You have so cunningly discharg'd your parts,
That while we live, rest confident you shall
Command *Dinant* and *Cleremont*; nor *Beaupre*,
Nor *Verdone* scents it: for the Ladies, they
Were easie to be gull'd.

1 Gent. 'Twas but a jest,
And yet the jest may chance to break our necks
Should it be known.

Cler. Fear nothing.

Din. Cleremont,
Say, what success?

Cler. As thou wouldst wish, 'tis done Lad,

The grove will witness with me, that this night
I lay not like a block: but how speed you?

Din. I yet am in suspence, devise some means
To get these off, and speedily.

Cler. I have it,
Come, we are dull, I think that the good fellows,
Our predecessors in this place, were not
So foolish, and improvident husbands, but
'Twill yield us meat and wine.

1 Gent. Let's ransack it,
'Tis ours now by the Law.

Cler. How say you sweet one,
Have you an appetite?

Ana. To walk again
I'th' Woods, if you think fit, rather than eat.

Cler. A little respite prethee; nay blush not,
You ask but what's your own, and warrantable:
Monsieur, Beaupre, Verdone,
What think you of the motion?

Verd. Lead the way.

Beau. We follow willingly.   [*Ex. Man.* Din. *and* Lam.

Cler. When you shall think fit,
We will expect you.

Din. Now be mistris of
Your promise Lady.

Lam. 'Twas to give you hearing.

Din. But that word hearing, did include a grant,
And you must make it good.

Lam. Must?

Din. Must and shall,
I will be fool'd no more, you had your tricks;
Made properties of me, and of my friend;
Presum'd upon your power, and whip'd me with
The rod of mine own dotage: do not flatter
Your self with hope, that any humane help
Can free you, and for aid by miracle
A base unthankfull woman is unworthy.

Lam. You will not force me?

Din. Rather than enjoy you
With your consent, because I will torment you;
I'le make you feel the effects of abus'd love,
And glory in your torture.

Lam. Brother, Nephew,
Help, help, for Heavens sake.

Din. Tear your throat, cry louder,
Though every leaf, these trees bear, were an Echo,
And summon'd in your best friends to redeem you,
It should be fruitless: 'tis not that I love you,
Or value those delights you prize so high,
That I'le enjoy you, a French crown will buy
More sport, and a companion, to whom,
You in your best trim are an Ethiop.

Lam. Forbear me then.

Din. Not so, I'le do't in spite,
And break that stubborn disobedient will,
That hath so long held out, that boasted honour
I will make equal with a common Whores;
The spring of Chastity, that fed your pride,
And grew into a River of vain glory,
I will defile with mudd, the mudd of lust,
And make it loathsome even to goats.

Lam. O Heaven!
No pity Sir?

Din. You taught me to be cruel,

And dare you think of mercy? I'le tell thee fool,
Those that surpriz'd thee, were my instruments,
I can plot too good Madam, you shall find it:
And in the stead of licking of my fingers,
Kneeling and whining like a boy new breech'd,
To get a toy forsooth, not worth an apple,
Thus make my way, and with Authority
Command what I would have.

Lam. I am lost for ever:
Good Sir, I do confess my fault, my gross fault,
And yield my self up, miserable guilty;
Thus kneeling I confess, you cannot study
Sufficient punishments to load me with;
I am in your power, and I confess again,
You cannot be too cruel: if there be,
Besides the loss of my long guarded honour,
Any thing else to make the ballance even,
Pray put it in, all hopes, all helpes have left me;
I am girt round with sorrow, hell's about me,
And ravishment the least that I can look for,
Do what you please.

Din. Indeed I will do nothing,
Nor touch nor hurt you Lady, nor had ever
Such a lewd purpose.

Lam. Can there be such goodness,
And in a man so injur'd?

Din. Be confirm'd in't.
I seal it thus: I must confess you vex'd me,
In fooling me so often, and those fears
You threw upon me call'd for a requital,
Which now I have return'd, all unchast love
Dinant thus throws away; live to man-kind,
As you have done to me, and I will honour
Your vertue, and no more think of your beauty.

Lam. All I possess, comes short of satisfaction.

Din. No complements: the terrours of this night
Imagine but a fearfull dream, and so

With ease forget it: for *Dinant*, that labour'd
To blast your honour, is a Champion for it,
And will protect and guard it.

Lam. 'Tis as safe then,
As if a compleat Army undertook it.   [*Exeunt.*

   Enter La-writ, Sampson, *Clyents.*

La-writ. Do not perswade me gentle Monsieur *Sampson*,
I am a mortal man again, a Lawyer,
My martiall part I have put off.

Sam. Sweet Monsieur,
Let but our honours teach us.

La-writ. Monsieur *Sampson*,
My honourable friend, my valiant friend,
Be but so beaten, forward my brave Clients,
I am yours, and you are mine again, be but so thrasht,
Receive that Castigation with a cudgel.

Sam. Which calls upon us for a Reparation.

La-writ. I have, it cost me half a crown, I bear it
All over me, I bear it Monsieur *Sampson*;
The oyls, and the old woman that repairs to me,
To 'noint my beaten body.

Sam. It concerns you,
You have been swing'd.

La-writ. Let it concern thee too;
Goe and be beaten, speak scurvy words, as I did,
Speak to that Lion Lord, waken his anger,
And have a hundred Bastinado's, doe;
Three broken pates, thy teeth knockt out, do *Sampson*,
Thy valiant arms and leggs beaten to Poultesses,
Do silly *Sampson*, do.

1 Cly. You wrong the Gentleman,
To put him out of his right mind thus:
You wrong us, and our Causes.

La-writ. Down with him Gentlemen,
Turn him, and beat him, if he break our peace,
Then when thou hast been Lam'd, thy small guts perisht,
Then talk to me, before I scorn thy counsel,
Feel what I feel, and let my Lord repair thee.

Sam. And can the brave *La-writ*—

2 Cly. Tempt him no further,
Be warn'd and say no more.

La-writ. If thou doest, *Sampson,*
Thou seest my Mirmidons, I'le let 'em loose,
That in a moment—

Sam. I say nothing, Sir, but I could wish—

La-writ. They shall destroy thee wishing;
There's ne'r a man of these, but have lost ten causes,
Dearer then ten mens lives; tempt, and thou diest:
Goe home, and smile upon my Lord, thine Uncle,
Take Mony of the men thou mean'st to Cousin,
Drink Wine, and eat good meat, and live discreetly,
Talk little, 'tis an antidote against a beating;
Keep thy hand from thy sword, and from thy Laundress placket,
And thou wilt live long.

1 Cly. Give ear, and be instructed.

La-writ. I find I am wiser than a Justice of Peace now,
Give me the wisdom that's beaten into a man
That sticks still by him: art thou a new man?

Sam. Yes, yes,
Thy learned precepts have inchanted me.

La-writ. Goe my son *Sampson,* I have now begot thee,
I'le send thee causes; speak to thy Lord, and live,
And lay my share by, goe and live in peace,
Put on new suits, and shew fit for thy place;
That man neglects his living, is an Asse: [*Exit* Samp.
Farewel; come chearily boyes, about our business,
Now welcom tongue again, hang Swords.

1 Cly. Sweet Advocate.   [*Exeunt.*

   Enter Nurse, *and* Charlote.

Nur. I know not wench, they may call 'em what they will,
Outlawes, or thieves, but I am sure, to me
One was an honest man, he us'd me well,
What I did, 'tis no matter, he complain'd not.

Char. I must confess, there was one bold with me too,
Some coy thing would say rude, but 'tis no matter,
I was to pay a Waiting womans ransom,
And I have don't, and I would pay't again,
Were I ta'n to morrow.

Nur. Alas, there was no hurt,
If 't be a sin for such as live at hard meat,
And keep a long Lent, in the woods as they do,
To taste a little flesh.

Char. God help the Courtiers,
That lye at rack and manger.

Nur. I shall love
A thief the better for this while I live,
They are men of a charitable vocation,
And give where there is need, and with discretion,
And put a good speed penny in my purse,
That has been empty twenty years.

Char. Peace Nurse,
Farewel, and cry not rost meat, me thinks *Cleremont*
And my Lady *Anabel* are in one night,
Familiarly acquainted.

Nur. I observe it,
If she have got a penny too.

   Enter Vertaign, Champernel, *and* Provost.

Charl. No more,
My Lord Monsieur *Vertaigne*, the provost too,
Haste and acquaint my Lady.   [*Ex. Nur. and* Char.

Pro. Wonderous strange.

Vert. 'Tis true Sir, on my credit.

Cham. O mine honour.

Pro. I have been provost-Marshal twenty years,
And have trussed up a thousand of these rascals,
But so near *Paris* yet I never met with
One of that Brotherhood.

Cham. We to our cost have,
But will you search the wood?

Pro. It is beset,
They cannot scape us, nothing makes me wonder,
So much as having you within their power
They let you goe; it was a Courtesy,
That French thieves use not often, I much pity
The Gentle Ladies, yet I know not how,
I rather hope than fear.

    Enter Dinant, Cleremont, Verdone, Beaupre, Lamira, Anabel,
    Charlote, *Nurse.*

Are these the prisoners?

Din. We were such.

Verd. Kill me not, excess of joy.

Cham. I see thou livest, but hast thou had no foul play?

Lam. No on my soul, my usage hath been noble,
Far from all violence.

Cham. How were you freed?
But kiss me first, we'l talk of that at leasure,
I am glad I have thee; Niece how you keep off,
As you knew me not?

Ana. Sir, I am where
I owe most duty.

Cler. 'Tis indeed most true Sir,
The man that should have been your bedfellow
Your Lordships bedfellow, that could not smell out
A Virgin of sixteen, that was your fool,
To make you merry, this poor simple fellow
Has met the maid again, and now she knows
He is a man.

Cham. How! is she dishonoured?

Cler. Not unless marriage be dishonourable,
Heaven is a witness of our happy contract,
And the next Priest we meet shall warrant it
To all the world: I lay with her in jeast,
'Tis turn'd to earnest now.

Cham. Is this true, Niece?

Din. Her blushing silence grants it; nay Sir storm not,
He is my friend, and I can make this good,
His birth and fortunes equal hers, your Lordship
Might have sought out a worse, we are all friends too,
All differences end thus. Now Sir, unless
You would raise new dissentions, make perfect
What is so well begun.

Vert. That were not manly.

Lam. Let me perswade you.

Cham. Well God give you joy,
She shall not come a Begger to you Sir.
For you Monsieur *Dinant* 'ere long I'le shew you
Another Niece, to this not much inferiour,
As you shall like proceed.

Din. I thank you Sir.

Cham. Back then to *Paris*: well that travel ends
That makes of deadly enemies perfect friends.
   [*Exeunt omnes.*

Epilogue.

Gentlemen,

I am sent forth to enquire what you decree }
Of us and of our Poets, they will be }
This night exceeding merry, so will we }
If you approve their labours. They profess
You are their Patrons, and we say no less,
Resolve us then, for you can only tell
Whether we have done id'ly or done well.

APPENDIX

Page numbering refers to the original publication only

THE LITTLE FRENCH LAWYER.

p. 373, ll. 3-40. Not in 1st folio.

p. 374, l. 2. 2nd folio *misprints*] aud.
 l. 25. 2nd folio *misprints*] Frcenh.
 l. 27. And banisht.
 l. 35. Will you? and yet—.
 l. 37. Mistris, feathers.

p. 375, l. 30. godly.

p. 378, l. 8. Epithalamin.
 l. 21. for 'twill be.

p. 379, l. 15. Upon a.
 l. 23. tempest.
 l. 39. *Omits* and.

p. 382, l. 22. 2nd folio *misprints*] by.
 l. 33. *Transfers* to *to beginning of next line.*

p. 383, l. 16. 2nd folio] their.
 l. 36. parts.

p. 384, l. 2. 2nd folio] beween.

p. 385, l. 25. On my.

p. 386, l. 8. make rise.

p. 387, l. 36. Those dedicates.

p. 388, l. 30. Lewis eleventh.

p. 389, l. 3. you persev'd.
 l. 19. danger or.
 l. 33. *A comma has been inserted at the end of the line.*

p. 390, l. 4. honours.
 l. 5. suffer.
 l. 9. loose.

p. 391, l. 8. to this.

p. 392, l. 1. up you.
 l. 3. 2nd folio *misprints*] pecies.
 l. 17. If you.

p. 394, l. 33. 2nd folio] Avocate.

p. 396, l. 14. Beau, *instead of* Cler.
 l. 20. what a.

p. 397, l. 18. *Omits stage direction.*
 l. 36. loose.

p. 398, l. 5. What master.
 l. 27. Cock a two.
 l. 37. makes all this plaine.

p. 399, l. 3. 2nd folio *misprints*] Bur.
 l. 19. 2nd folio] thow.
 l. 34. *Omits* singing *in stage direction.*

p. 400, l. 16. my whole.

p. 401, l. 13. Declare that.
 l. 27. And hunny out your.
 l. 31. 2nd folio *misprints*] my.

p. 404, l. 17. 2nd folio *misprints*] imfamie.

p. 405, l. 39. *Omits* not.

p. 406, l. 7. In our.

p. 409, l. 27. going lesse.

p. 411, l. 9. ye did.
 l. 29. Pray.
 l. 36. *Omits* do.

p. 412, l. 1. any corner.
  l. 5. the louer.
  l. 35. laughters.

p. 413, l. 10. y'are? Gentleman.
  l. 15. hate.
  l. 17. for my.
  l. 22. and carriage ... calls.
  l. 35. your.

p. 414, l. 24. Hee is.

p. 415, l. 4. will make.
  l. 12. Why, to it.
  l. 21. wake.
  l. 38. Slaves feed.

p. 416, l. 19. 'ore.
  l. 28. a meane.

p. 417, l. 6. *Adds stage direction*] Wine.
  l. 8. doe but kisse.
  l. 11. Will you.
  l. 28. *Adds stage direction*] Recorders.

p. 418, l. 37. thou knowest.

p. 419, l. 4. quarter.
  l. 12. Madman, a fool ... shew thee man.
  l. 14. No I'le.
  l. 32. no flame.

p. 420, l. 40. point you.

p. 424, l. 16. 2nd folio *misprints*] dies.

p. 425, l. 29. 2nd folio *misprints*] Cler.

p. 427, l. 5. *Adds stage direction*] Put off.

p. 428, l. 32. Firsts, seconds, thirds.

p. 429, l. 1. p— — on't.

l. 27. still devising.

p. 431, l. 19. *Gives this line to* Lam.
 l. 22. *Adds as though a stage direction*] Now.
 l. 31. *Reads* My legs in my good house, my Armour on.

p. 432, l. 12. yet are, if men.

p. 435, l. 12. *Reads*] *La-wr.* Bee't then. | Mens fates, etc.
 ll. 15 and 16. *Gives these two lines to* Sam.
 l. 18. 2nd folio] Vertagine.
 l. 23. Strike.
 l. 25. Gives No, no, ... not *to Verta*.

p. 439, l. 11. Corvina.
 l. 34. loose.

p. 440, l. 1. Quinti.
 l. 3. the Chamber doore.

p. 441, l. 16. 2nd folio] vills.

p. 444, l. 27. hand of heaven.

p. 445, l. 24. *Omits* is.

p. 448, l. 4. *Omits* Din. *by mistake and prints* enjury *for* enjoy.

p. 449, l. 35. My mortall.

p. 450, l. 36. mine Uncle.

Lightning Source UK Ltd.
Milton Keynes UK
UKHW042047051222
413454UK00008B/53